Asian Favourites Made Plant-based

more than veggies

JOY YUAN

Marshall Cavendish
Cuisine

To the best people
I've ever met.

Editor: Lo Yi Min
Designer: Bernard Go Kwang Meng

Copyright © 2020 Marshall Cavendish International (Asia) Private Limited

Published by Marshall Cavendish Cuisine
An imprint of Marshall Cavendish International

A member of the
Times Publishing Group

Other Marshall Cavendish Offices:
Marshall Cavendish Corporation, 800 Westchester Ave, Suite N-641, Rye Brook, NY 10573, USA • Marshall Cavendish International (Thailand) Co Ltd, 253 Asoke, 16th Floor, Sukhumvit 21 Road, Klongtoey Nua, Wattana, Bangkok 10110, Thailand • Marshall Cavendish (Malaysia) Sdn Bhd, Times Subang, Lot 46, Subang Hi-Tech Industrial Park, Batu Tiga, 40000 Shah Alam, Selangor Darul Ehsan, Malaysia

Marshall Cavendish is a registered trademark of Times Publishing Limited

National Library Board, Singapore Cataloguing in Publication Data

Name(s): Yuan, Joy.
Title: More than veggies : Asian favourites made plant-based / Joy Yuan.
Description: Singapore : Marshall Cavendish Cuisine, [2020]
Identifier(s): OCN 1176314123 | 978-981-48-9337-4 (paperback)
Subject(s): LCSH: Vegan Cooking. | Vegetarian Cooking. | Cooking, Asian. | LCGFT: Cookbooks.
Classification: DDC 641.5636--dc23

Printed in Singapore

contents

acknowledgements

Here are the people who made my first book possible:

My parents, who went out of their way to ensure that I grew up with the most delicious vegetarian foods, and who have firmly supported me in creating this book.

My vegan and non-vegan friends, who would make my day by sharing how excited they were while the book was still in production and enthusiastically pre-ordering it.

The readers of my blog and social media pages, who are always with me. Making free, quality content is never easy, but your messages of support always give me a sense of accomplishment and spur me on in sharing helpful content about plant-based eating.

My first and only photography teacher, Mr James, who always made his classes interesting, engaging and hands-on.

Singapore's tight-knit vegan community, whose members always have each other's back.

The amazing people from Marshall Cavendish who worked on this book and guided me patiently along the way.

And finally, my other half, who cheered me on all the time from afar.

introduction

So you've decided to eat more plants — that's great, but what's next? Will the meals that you eat from now on be enjoyable, comforting and accessible, without burning a hole in your pocket?

The rising popularity of plant-based diets in the recent years is a wonderful surprise that has made plant-based eating much easier. Yet, at the start of my food journey, I couldn't help but notice the lack of representation of Asian cuisines in the international plant-based scene. As I couldn't find recipes of my favourite dishes, I tried making my own.

My tried and tested results are now here in your hands. This book offers 45 recipes of Southeast and South Asian flavours that you can make at home. Who would have thought that favourites like rendang, dumplings, *kaya* and pandan cake can be made without animal-based ingredients? What's more, these plant-based versions aren't a huge jump in taste from their originals.

Making these recipes accessible is very important to me, as I grew up vegetarian and subsequently went vegan at age 18. The feeling of alienation from not being included is something all too familiar to me. Throughout the book, I've included recommendations for making gluten-free, soy-free and allium-free substitutions — these have been indicated with helpful icons at the start of each recipe. Do read the notes for each recipe to get ideas for alternatives. Moreover, the dishes are made from mainly common pantry items, such as grains, beans, lentils, herbs and spices, as well as tofu, tempeh and vegetables. If you don't like any particular ingredient, feel free to try alternatives. Make the dishes yours! If you have questions about replacing anything, reach out to me @morethanveggies.

I hope you enjoy this collection as much as I do, and that these recipes will become part of your home cooking repertoire to make life easier and healthier for you!

Joy Yuan

pantry items

<u>Nuts</u>

Cashews and peanuts (essential)

Cashews and peanuts are commonly used in Southeast Asian cuisine. They are versatile nuts with healthy fats, and can be made crunchy by roasting or frying, or soft by braising. Avoid them if you have nut allergies.

White sesame seeds (good to have)

When roasted, these give a subtle sweet and nutty aroma that can uplift your dish. I often use it as a finishing ingredient or topping. White sesame seeds are generally more fragrant than their black counterpart, thus you'll find that the recipes here don't call for the latter.

Flaxseed powder (good to have)

A superfood, this is not a traditional ingredient but highly recommended for binding purposes. Mix flaxseed powder with water using a 1:3 ratio (1 Tbsp flaxseed powder + 3 Tbsp water) and set it aside for 10 minutes; it becomes a viscous liquid that's almost like egg whites. It produces a fantastic binding effect while being rather flavourless. In this book, it's essential in the tempeh *bak kwa* recipe.

<u>Flours</u>

All-purpose flour (essential)

Also known as plain flour, this is highly versatile and very commonly used in Asian recipes, like my family's dumplings. Feel free to use superfine wholewheat flour in place if you like.

Wholewheat flour (essential)

Wholewheat flour is not as processed as all-purpose flour, making it more nutritious. It also produces a denser texture, a much darker brown appearance, and a nutty, wheat-y aftertaste, which may or may not be desirable. To make a dish healthier, sometimes we mix 50% all-purpose flour with 50% wholewheat flour.

Cornstarch (good to have)

This has no taste on its own and is used for thickening soups and sauces in Chinese cuisine to produce a more concentrated flavour. It's also added when the dish needs a slight binding effect or a light glossy finish.

<u>Proteins</u>

Canned chickpeas (essential)

Not only are chickpeas high in protein and other nutrients, but the liquid that they are cooked in (which canned chickpeas come with) is also a pantry staple! Known as aquafaba, it is a versatile egg replacer in many sweet and savoury recipes.

Dried soybeans or other beans (good to have)

In addition to canned beans, I recommend stocking up on dried beans. You can get more flavours and nutrients from cooking dried beans. You can also stew them for very long without them turning mushy. Dried beans should be soaked for at least 10 hours before use for faster cooking and easier digestion.

Lentils (essential)

Like beans, lentils are legumes, but they are smaller, have a lens-like shape and are usually without an outer skin. Some lentils are split versions of beans. They cook faster but to a mushier texture, which is great for uses like making breaded croquettes.

Quinoa (essential)

Not only is this a source of complete protein (containing all nine essential amino acids), it also can be an alternative to grains if cooked right. Fun fact: it's actually not a grain but a seed! If you are new to quinoa, I recommend starting with white quinoa as it cooks faster and has a softer texture.

Seitan (good to have)

Seitan is basically a block of flour-based protein with most of the starch removed. Traditionally used in Chinese and Japanese cuisines, it's valued for its meaty and chewy texture. It can replace tofu, tempeh and mushrooms in many recipes.

Tofu (essential)

Tofu comes in many types, but mainly two types are called for in this book: soft and firm tofu. Soft tofu is pudding-like and fragile, so it has to be handled with care. It is used in tofu scrambles and as a high-protein addition to soups. As soft tofu contains a lot of moisture, drain it by letting it sit on a sieve for 5 minutes. Firm tofu is easier to handle and can be pressed to extract some moisture if you prefer a drier and even firmer texture.

Fried tofu puffs (good to have)

Also known as *tau pok*, this has a light spongy texture, which allows it to absorb sauces superbly. Before using these, I usually rinse off the excess oil as these are deep-fried.

Dried beancurd skin (good to have)

This is not tofu but the skin formed on the surface when boiling soy milk. Called *yuba* in Japan, it's collected and dried into sheets. They should be soaked before use to soften.

Tempeh (essential)

This is a block of fermented soybean which originates from Indonesia. Compared to tofu, it has better digestibility and higher fibre. It can absorb flavours better than tofu due to its higher porosity. However, tempeh has a certain pungency. Steaming or boiling it for 3–5 minutes before using helps remove that. Strong flavours can also be used to mask it, which is why traditional tempeh recipes use plenty of spices.

Carbs

Brown / White rice (essential)

Rice is a staple in Asian cuisines. There are many different types, e.g. Japanese, Thai, basmati, etc. I encourage you to use your favourite to make your dishes more enjoyable. I enjoy brown rice, thus I used it in recipes here.

Yellow noodles (good to have)

Yellow noodles are thick round noodles made with flour, yellow colouring and, traditionally, lye water. This is often used in Chinese dishes like claypot noodles and Hokkien mee. Because it's more alkaline than other noodles, it withstands cooking well and absorbs more flavour while maintaining a chewy and springy texture. However, it may have a slight bitter aftertaste, which is why adding a bit of lime or lemon juice to the dish at the end helps reduce that. Pasta may be an alternative to this in a pinch.

Rice noodles (essential)

Rice noodles are less chewy than wheat noodles. They work well in dishes that are not stewed or braised for long as the noodles can break easily. If you are avoiding wheat, these are a good alternative, but avoid overcooking them.

Wheat noodles (essential)

This is another staple of many Asian cuisines and my favourite carbohydrate. There are many different types, thin, flat, thick — experiment to find your favourite. As a general rule of thumb, thinner noodles need the least time to cook, thick ones need the most time. I've shared my family's handmade noodle recipe on page 31.

Vegetables

Ready-to-eat seaweed (essential)

There are a variety of these and they are great as toppings on soups, noodles or rice. They add an extra boost of ocean-y umami and iodine to your dish.

Kelp (essential)

This is dried seaweed that must be cooked before eating, and some are specially made for soups. It must be soaked beforehand to soften, and the soaking water can be used as a soup base. I recommend using kelp from Japan as it is often the cleanest and without any sand. It is also known as kombu.

Wakame (essential)

This is young seaweed bud and it usually comes dried. Much more tender and smaller than kelp, it also cooks faster. I love dropping 4–5 pieces into miso soup, and using it to give a briny umami to dishes that originally use shrimp or other seafood as the main flavour.

Chinese mountain yam (good to have)

Also known as *nagaimo* or *shan yao*, it's a staple in both Japanese and Chinese cuisines. In Chinese cuisine it's usually cooked, but in Japanese cuisine it's eaten raw. I mainly use it as an egg replacer when binding and moisture are needed. When grated, it acts as a superb binder.

Mushrooms

Shiitake mushrooms (essential)

Knowing how to use both dried and fresh shiitake will greatly elevate your dishes! Fresh shiitake are more tender than rehydrated ones, but they have a milder flavour. Thus I use them for stir-fries and sautéed dishes where the mushroom flavour doesn't need to be too pronounced. When shiitake are dried, their woody and umami flavours are concentrated. Before using, rinse and soak in water first; the soaking water can be used as a base for soups and sauces. Use the rehydrated mushrooms as you would fresh ones.

Monkeyhead mushrooms (good to have)

This is rarer than shiitake and really a gem. It's flavourless but incredibly meaty in texture that many are surprised that it's a mushroom! Also known as lion's mane mushroom, this usually comes frozen or dried. I prefer using frozen ones as dried ones need a lot more preparation to rid it of its natural bitterness. Note that some frozen ones contain egg.

Oyster mushrooms (good to have)

These are milder than shiitake and easy to prepare — simply tear them into smaller pieces, no cutting needed. They are great in almost anything because the mushroom flavour doesn't overpower other ingredients. Adding one or two more mushrooms to your repertoire will surely bring your dishes to another level.

King oyster mushrooms (good to have)

This bulbous, thick and meaty mushroom can withstand cooking well and doesn't shrink too much, so it soaks up lots of flavours. I love slicing it thinly so it cooks to a tender texture.

Wood's Ear Fungus (good to have)

I disliked this when I was a kid because I found the texture a bit strange, but I was always made to eat it for it is high in iron. Now I love it for its refreshing crunchiness! Its mild flavour also allows for endless creativity. This is available fresh or dried.

Condiments

Chinese preserved radish (good to have)

Preserved vegetables are pantry essentials in Chinese households. The Cantonese name of this is *chai poh*. It is sweet and salty preserved radish bits that are used in a multitude of dishes. They are big on umami and have a crunchy texture. They can also be a flavourful substitute for alliums if you don't take alliums.

Chinese preserved mustard (good to have)

Also known as *zha cai*, this is a type of pickled mustard that's wetter than preserved radish. It is used in a variety of Chinese comfort foods. There are many variations: some are mild, and some are spicy, so experiment to find what you love!

Regular / Light / Premium soy sauces (essential)

Soy sauce, the all-purpose seasoning, is appealing because it's associated with umami, or lip-smacking savoury taste. Regular soy sauce is made using two methods; fermentation, which usually takes six months; or chemical hydrolysis, which takes a few days. I recommend buying naturally fermented soy sauce for the best flavour.

Premium soy sauce is grade-A soy sauce that has an incredibly tasty and complex flavour, probably due to premium beans being used and a longer fermentation period. It is pricier than usual soy sauces, but worth having.

Light soy sauce is less rich than regular soy sauce due to less fermentation. It's great in light stir-fries or for times when you need saltiness and just a bit of flavour without changing the dish's colour or flavour too much. It can be used interchangeably with regular soy sauce.

Dark soy sauce (essential)

Dark soy sauce is traditionally used to braise meats and make sauces, stews and gravies. It is richer, sweeter and thicker than other soy sauces. It's added to noodles and protein dishes to develop a rich and deep colour.

Sweet soy sauce (good to have)

Sweet soy sauce is popular in Southeast Asian countries. Also known as *kecap manis*, it is soy sauce mixed with palm sugar, making it thick and sticky. It is often used in fried noodles, rice dishes and sauces to give a sweet aftertaste. You can make your own by boiling equal parts palm sugar and dark soy sauce together and reducing the mixture until it is thick enough to coat a spoon.

Tamari / Liquid aminos (good to have)

Both are gluten-free alternatives to regular soy sauce, which almost always contains gluten. Tamari is traditional wheat-free Japanese soy sauce, while liquid aminos look and taste similar to soy sauce, and are usually made from soybeans or rice. If you are on a gluten-free diet, these two options are highly recommended.

Fermented beancurd (essential)

Sometimes called the Chinese version of cheese, it's simply fermented tofu and comes in many variations. It does have a salty, cheese-like flavour, with a texture quite similar to cream cheese. Often eaten as an accompaniment to porridge, this can also be used to give umami to sauces or soups.

Fermented bean paste (essential)

In many Asian cuisines, some form of fermented soybean paste is often used. *Tau cheo*, the Chinese one, is used more often in the recipes here. Unlike the smoother Japanese miso or Korean gochujang, this contains almost-whole beans. It is highly versatile and great with most veggies or proteins.

Fermented dried black beans (good to have)

This is made from black soybeans, giving it is dark colour. It has a bolder flavour than *tau cheo*. Drier compared to the other bean pastes, it needs a bit of liquid to help carry the umami throughout the dish. It's great in almost all dishes, ranging from noodles to stir-fries.

Miso (essential)

Widely used in Japanese cuisine for its intense umami, this is soybeans fermented with *koji*, a rice starter. It also comes in many variations, like white, red and brown. I prefer white miso as it's milder, more easily available and goes well with almost everything.

Chinese black vinegar (essential)

Unlike other vinegars, this is strong and bold. It is made from fermenting wheat with other grains. Just a few drops can add an appetising tang and boost umami greatly. For a gluten-free similar alternative, mix 1:1 balsamic vinegar with rice vinegar.

Sesame oil (essential)

This refers to Chinese roasted sesame oil, not the pale yellow sesame oil used for cooking. This oil is mainly used as a seasoning; just a few drops after cooking makes a fragrant addition to your dishes.

Vanilla paste (essential)

I prefer vanilla paste over extracts or flavourings. Vanilla paste has specks of seeds and smells absolutely amazing. Since we are baking without eggs and dairy products, any chance to impart more flavour should be seized!

Lime / Lemon (essential)

In Southeast Asian cooking, lime (specifically calamansi lime) is commonly squeezed into dishes for an extra oomph and tang. The fruity sourness works fantastic with bold spices. Lemon can be a good substitute.

<u>Spices and Herbs</u>

Galangal (good to have)

This looks similar to ginger but it's very different! Much less spicy and more citrusy than ginger, it is commonly used in Thai, Malay and Indonesian cooking. Because galangal is rather hard, it should be sliced, not grated.

Ginger (essential)

I feel that ginger is underrated. It's got strong characteristics on its own that changes depending on how it's used or combined with different ingredients. It can be used in almost anything from soups to stir-fries. When using it to replace alliums in a stir-fry, simply sauté it just like you would with onions or garlic. Use it at the start of cooking before adding other ingredients to infuse your oil or liquid with its fragrance.

Kaffir lime leaves (good to have)

These look similar to bay leaves but are much more citrusy and fragrant. Often used in Southeast Asian cuisines for curries and stir-fries, just one or two leaves can give a lingering bright and citrusy flavour. To use, crumple or tear with your hands to release its fragrance. This is difficult to substitute due to its unique fragrance, but freshly grated lemon or lime zest (avoid the white pith) can work to a certain extent.

Lemongrass (essential)

An important spice in Southeast Asian cooking, lemongrass has a gentle lingering lemon scent. It's used mainly as a base in curry pastes. It is very fibrous, so it can be a little tricky to work with. The trick is to bruise it with the back of a knife before slicing it to release the fragrance.

Pandan leaves (essential)

Think of this as a Southeast Asian vanilla. We use it to make both savoury and sweet foods, but more commonly sweet dishes. Those who grew up in Southeast Asia can relate to its sweet, creamy scent lingering in the air after the rain or wafting from neighbourhood bakeries. To use, either juice or tie the leaves into a knot. Due to its unique fragrance, it can't be easily replaced.

Tamarind paste (good to have)

This is a paste with a fruity, plum-like flavour that comes from the tamarind fruit. Traditionally used in many Asian curries to liven up a dish with its bold tang. It can be replaced with lime or lemon in a pinch.

Toon paste (good to have)

A great alternative if you don't take alliums. Sometimes called Chinese mahogany, Chinese cedar or *xiang chun*,

this is the best for imparting an onion flavour. To me, its flavour is about 70% similar to that of onions, just slightly more floral and without the pungency. I've never seen fresh Chinese toon sold in Southeast Asia as it spoils easily; it comes as a sauce or frozen paste. Use it as you would onions — sauté before adding other ingredients.

Five-spice powder (essential)

Chinese five-spice powder is a classic blend of star anise, cinnamon, Sichuan peppercorn, clove and fennel. Often used in meat dishes to bring out a meaty flavour, it works the same for proteins like tofu, tempeh and seitan too!

Star anise (good to have)

This distinctly sweet and aromatic spice is quite similar to liquorice. Because of its strong taste, it should only be used in small quantities. It works fantastically with proteins, citruses and alliums.

Asafoetida (good to have)

A common spice used in Indian cuisine, this comes from tree sap that has been dried and ground. It tastes very similar to onion and leek, so if you don't eat alliums due to non-religious reasons, it is a great substitute. Note that some religions consider this as part of five pungent vegetables that devotees should avoid. Those with gluten allergies should use gluten-free ones.

Non-dairy Milks

Unsweetened soy milk (essential)

Traditionally, soy milk is used in savoury dishes in China and Japan. Not only does it thicken soups and stews, it also gives a creamy texture while boosting savouriness by adding extra protein. It goes great with soy sauce and miso, and works excellently in baking. As it may separate under direct heat, always add

it into the dish last after removing from heat. As a general rule, use one that has higher fat content for cooking and baking. Oat or almond milk can be a soy-free alternative that gives a nutty flavour.

Coconut milk (essential)

This is a traditional staple in Asian cooking, used to thicken and enrich curries. It's also fantastic in plant-based baking as it has the highest fat content among plant milks. In baking, when eggs and dairy are omitted, we need to make up for the fat they provide to get the same level of richness and flavour. If you have health concerns, use soy, almond or oat milk.

Barista non-dairy milk (essential)

Not every plant milk can be frothed up like dairy milk, and that's where barista non-dairy milks come it. These are formulated to froth up perfectly. I find that they also add another layer of richness, so you can also enjoy them without any frothing. They are available in soy, oat or almond milk variations. Experiment to find your favourite!

Sweeteners

Gula Melaka (essential)

This is also called palm sugar or coconut palm sugar. It is used to sweeten traditional Southeast Asian cakes (*kueh*) and desserts, and is usually sold as a syrup, powdered or in blocks. Its richer and smokier flavour is comparable to brown sugar and molasses, so those can make a passable substitute.

Maltose syrup (good to have)

This is a sticky traditional Chinese syrup made from grains like corn and sometimes wheat. Its mild taste makes it versatile; it is used in savoury dishes and confectionery. It gives a characteristic glossiness to barbecued dishes. To replace, use sugar syrups, though you might not get a similar glossy effect.

Others

Baking soda (essential)

This does not help your baked good expand horizontally, but it gives a good rising effect. It is about thee to four times more effective than baking powder in creating lift in baked goods. More baking soda in a recipe does not equal to more lift or fluffiness. Too much baking soda gives a soapy aftertaste.

Baking powder (essential)

Baking powder is actually baking soda plus cream of tartar and sometimes a starch. It gives less lift than baking soda, which makes it easier to control. It helps cakes rise and expand horizontally. In eggless cooking and baking, this can be a good egg substitute when combined with vinegar and other ingredients.

Shredded coconut (essential)

This is dried coconut flesh (the white part) shredded into bits. It is often used in Southeast Asian dishes, from curries to confectionaries. In savoury dishes it can give a rich and nutty base flavour to overlay with spices and other flavours. In confectionery, it gives a subtle creamy sweetness and a bit of crunch for textural variation. Those who dislike strong coconut flavours, don't worry — this is much milder than coconut milk.

Black salt (essential)

Also known as *kala namak*, it's a salt that tastes like eggs! Since ancient times in India, this was used in Ayurvedic medicine. It's a unique salt that contains sulphur naturally, giving it a black or rusty pink colour. This is highly recommended if you miss eggy flavours or simply want to add extra oomph to your dishes. To retain the eggy taste, I recommend adding it after the dish has been removed from heat.

useful tools

Wok

A staple in a Chinese kitchen, this is usually made of material that's beaten thinly, so it transfers heat easily and cooks food very quickly. It can impart a unique smoky flavour to a dish.

Claypot

Food cooked in claypots loses little moisture and retains its flavours better. I prefer using a glazed claypot for easy cleaning up. To prevent any cracking, always start by heating the pot over low heat and increasing to medium after about 4–5 minutes. If your claypot is not well seasoned, use a bit of oil and more water during cooking to prevent burning.

Stock or soup pot

When a large volume of liquid boils, it tends to bubble upwards, so having a pot that is two or three times larger than what it contains is highly recommended.

Sieve

I recommend having at least three sieves: a deep, big one for noodles or for sifting large amounts of flour; a medium one to strain stock ingredients or sift flour, and a small one to locate specific items. These are also useful in draining excess liquid from ingredients like tofu.

Cheesecloth

For squeezing juices from ingredients or containing herbs and seasoning for stewing. Having these in the kitchen opens up plenty of culinary opportunities.

Long chopsticks

Using these reduces the risk of receiving hot oil splatters on your hand. Retrieving noodles from a pot is also easier.

Silicone spatula

This is more useful than wooden or metal spatulas, because it's flexible. It scrapes down the sides of bowls cleanly.

Balloon whisk

This is an important tool for mixing, as a spatula may push out too much air from the batter. I recommend having at least two of these so you don't have to keep washing it several times for one dish.

Electric mixer

Only an electric mixer can whip aquafaba well into stiff peaks. These usually come with other attachments like a dough kneader, which comes in handy too.

Blender

This works well with liquids. Extracting pandan juice must be done in a blender, as a food processor may not be able to fully break down every piece of pandan.

Food processor

This is better used for solids or to shorten time spent on tasks like chopping. Blending aromatics to make a curry paste works better in this as the blade's surface area is larger.

Mortar and pestle

To get the best flavour out of spices and herbs, pound with a mortar and pestle as it retains more of their aromatic oils. It can be used to mince garlic, ginger and more. So if you don't want to use a blender or food processor, try pounding these aromatics in small amounts.

basics

There are many commercially available curry pastes, but the best is still homemade as it's much fresher. This is a simple Chinese-style curry paste that uses any curry powder as a flavour base. Curry paste can be used not only in curry, but also in stir-fries, noodles, fried rice and more.

basic curry paste

Makes about 200 g

INGREDIENTS

3 stalks lemongrass, white part chopped finely, green part reserved

1.5-cm knob ginger, peeled and roughly chopped

2 shallots, peeled

6 candlenuts, halved

3 dried red chillies, seeds removed (add more if you like it spicier)

3 Tbsp curry powder (any type works)

2 tsp salt

7 Tbsp oil

METHOD

1. Pound together white part of lemongrass, ginger, shallots and dry ingredients in a mortar and pestle, then stir in oil. Alternatively, pulse everything together in a blender. If needed, add a couple tablespoonfuls of water to help the mixture blend.

2. Transfer paste to an airtight container. Keep refrigerated for up to 1 week.

3. To make curry with it, start by stir-frying paste with aromatics required in the curry recipe.

NOTES

- Allium-free option: you can omit the shallots and add more curry powder, ginger or lemongrass to compensate.

- Candlenuts are a waxy nut used in Southeast Asian cooking to thicken curries naturally. They can be substituted with macadamia nuts or cashews, although the effect is lessened. You can omit them for a thinner paste.

- Wear gloves while handling chillies. To remove the seeds quickly, slice chillies into halves and run under water to rinse the seeds off.

- Pounding the ingredients in a mortar and pestle is the best way to extract the aromatic oils. It takes more effort but your curry paste will be more fragrant.

Japanese mayonnaise is slightly sweeter and tangier then usual ones. It scores highly in the umami department as with many savoury Japanese condiments. It's used to top off okonomiyaki, takoyaki and many other dishes in modern Japanese cuisine. It's hard to find egg-free ones outside of Japan, so I made my own. This one is not made from soy milk or tofu, but aquafaba, the magical liquid that sits in a can of chickpeas!

japanese mayonnaise

Makes about 250 ml

INGREDIENTS

125 ml (¹/₂ cup) aquafaba

2 tsp mustard powder

500 ml (2 cups) neutral-tasting oil (avoid olive and coconut oil)

1 tsp black salt or regular salt

2 Tbsp sugar

2 tsp kelp (kombu) powder

A pinch of turmeric powder for colour (optional)

3 tsp rice vinegar

4 tsp fresh lemon juice

METHOD

1. Process aquafaba and mustard powder in a food processor.

2. Keep the food processor running while adding the subsequent ingredients. First, slowly drizzle in a third of the oil. Do not pour it in all at once.

3. Add salt, sugar and kelp powder. If using turmeric, add it in.

4. When the dry ingredients are mixed in, drizzle in another third of the oil.

5. Add rice vinegar and lemon juice, then drizzle in the remaining oil. After everything is combined, process the mixture for an extra 10 seconds.

6. Taste mayonnaise and adjust by adding more sugar, kelp powder or salt to your taste. Try not to add more of the liquid ingredients to avoid diluting it. If it's too thin, drizzle more oil while the food processor is running to thicken. Store in clean bottles. This can be kept refrigerated for a week.

NOTES

*   Step 2 involves emulsifying the oil, so that it can blend with the aquafaba properly. If you pour everything in at once, the two liquids will remain separated.

*   The purpose of kelp powder is to add umami without adding liquid that may disrupt the emulsifying process. Commercial ones usually contain a small amount of MSG. Kelp gives a briny umami that's highly celebrated in Japanese cuisine. Mushroom seasoning, vegan stock powder or cubes can be good alternatives too.

*   Black salt (*kala namak*) is recommended as it has a natural eggy taste. Regular salt can be used instead if black salt is not available.

*   Apple cider vinegar can be used instead of rice vinegar. Japanese mayonnaise doesn't contain distilled vinegar.

*   Extra virgin olive oil doesn't emulsify well at all, so avoid it at all costs!

*   Turmeric is only for colour, and thus optional. Do not use too much or its taste may come through.

2

sambal chilli

Makes 130 g

INGREDIENTS

1 tsp dried wakame

10 dried chillies, soaked in warm water for at least 30 minutes to soften, seeds removed

3–5 bird's eye chillies, sliced into halves, seeds removed

3 Tbsp oil

$1/2$ Tbsp fermented bean paste

3 Tbsp palm, coconut or white sugar

Juice from 5 calamansi limes

1 tsp salt

METHOD

1. In a pan, toast wakame over low heat for 1 minute until fragrant. Transfer to a mortar and pestle to pound until it resembles fine crumbs. Add dried and fresh chillies, then pound until you get a paste. Alternatively, process toasted wakame and chillies in a blender or food processor to get a thick paste. Add 2–3 tablespoonfuls of water to help the mixture blend.

2. In a wok or pan, heat oil over medium heat. Add chilli paste and fry for 1–2 minutes until fragrant. Add fermented bean paste, reduce the heat to low and cook while stirring continuously for about 15 minutes until oil seeps out. Chilli burns easily, so it's important to keep stirring. If you feel it's starting to burn, add a couple tablespoonfuls of water to avoid that.

3. Stir in sugar and cook until paste is smooth and shiny. Its colour will also darken due to caramelisation of the sugar.

4. Lastly, mix in lime juice and salt. Taste and adjust with more lime juice, salt or sugar. Let cool completely before storing in the refrigerator. It can be kept for up to 10 days in a clean airtight container. To keep for longer, freeze it.

NOTES

*   If you can take onion, garlic and shallots, I recommend adding these to your sambal for the most authentic flavour. This will also reduce the spiciness.

*   Wakame is optional as it simply gives a briny flavour that would have been imparted by shrimp paste. You can omit it if you like.

*   Sugar is quite important to balance out the spiciness while bringing out more flavours, so I don't recommend omitting it completely. You can reduce it if you are watching your sugar intake.

*   Lime and lemon can be used instead of calamansi lime. However, calamansi is still most suitable as its nuance and aroma matches the bold spices extremely well.

Growing up with Southeast Asian foods, you can't have too many sambal chilli recipes. Sambal chilli is a red chilli paste that serves as a condiment to many different dishes in Southeast Asia, especially in Indonesia, Malaysia and Singapore. This particular potent sambal chilli recipe is a basic plant-based one with only a few ingredients. You can dress it up with lemongrass, shallots, garlic, ginger and more! Try out different combinations to find your favourite. Calamansi lime may not be readily available outside of Southeast Asia, so lime or lemon can be used as a substitute. However, calamansi lime is best for sambal as it adds amazing aroma and nuance.

clear soup

Makes 2.5–3 litres

INGREDIENTS

4 litres (16 cups) water

2–3 pieces dried kelp (kombu), cleaned according to packet instructions

4–5 dried shiitake mushrooms, rinsed lightly to clean

$1/3$ cup red lentils, soaked for at least 30 minutes in warm water

1 carrot, chopped into 1-cm long pieces

1 corn, chopped into 3 parts

1 potato, peeled and cubed

1 stalk celery, chopped into 5-cm lengths

1-cm knob ginger, sliced

2 tsp salt, or to taste

A dash of ground white pepper

METHOD

1. Place water, kelp and shiitake in a pot. Bring to a boil over medium-low heat and remove kelp just before water begins to boil.

2. After the water comes to a boil, keep at medium-low heat and add lentils, carrot, corn, potato, celery and ginger.

3. Increase heat to medium-high, return mixture to a boil and simmer half covered for at least 40 minutes. Use a spoon to skim away any foam or impurities that gather on the surface.

4. Season with salt and pepper before straining soup into another large pot. Let cool completely before storing in the refrigerator. This can be kept for up to 5 days. To keep for longer, portion immediately and freeze.

NOTES

- Portion the soup and freeze in silicone bags or soft plastic containers. This way you can push out a block and plop it right into the pot when needed.

- For variations, you can use other veggies like radish, tomato, napa cabbage, snow peas, leek or onion. Sometimes my mother even adds an apple to sweeten the stock naturally.

- I don't recommend using fresh shiitake mushrooms here as dried ones have a more concentrated flavour.

- Traditional Chinese vegetarian clear soup has soybeans, but I used red lentils because of convenience. Soybeans have to be soaked overnight in advance and take much longer to cook. But feel free to try out different beans to find what works for you.

- Various bean pastes like miso or *tau cheo* can be used to salt this soup instead. Experiment to find your favourite combination!

Chinese clear soup is the accompaniment for many savoury dishes to cleanse the palate and offer a refreshing contrast. It's comforting and homely, a taste that many of us grew up with. Commonly made with chicken, I've added a twist to a traditional allium-free vegetarian recipe by including lentils and potato. Protein and starch boosts savouriness, so they make this veggie-based soup taste richer.

Noodles are my ultimate comfort food, and my favourite are the ones my father makes from scratch, with wholewheat flour added for extra nutrition. Rustic and imperfect, they catch sauce perfectly. They are nutty, springy, and extremely toothsome. To let the noodles shine, we keep the dressing and toppings simple. We boil them and toss with soy sauce, sesame oil and Chinese vinegar, then top them off generously with some chopped spring onions. Here's how my father makes these noodles.

traditional handmade noodles

Makes about 800 g

INGREDIENTS

500 g all-purpose flour
200 g wholewheat flour
1 tsp salt
250 ml (1 cup) water

METHOD

1. Sift flour into a large bowl and add salt. Add a third of the water at a time, mixing and kneading the mixture into a dough. Scrape down the sides and mix well until there is no more flour or residue sticking to the bowl's sides or your fingers.

2. Cover the bowl and let sit for at least 1 hour. The dough will reach its most ideal texture after 4–6 hours, when it feels soft while maintaining some springiness.

3. Have a bowl of flour on the side when rolling out the dough. Lightly flour a large, flat and clean surface.

4. Turn out dough and knead for 5–10 minutes, adding a small handful of flour if the dough sticks. Cut the dough into halves. We'll work on one half portion at a time.

5. Roll dough into a large rectangle or ellipse about 0.5-cm thick. Sprinkle a small handful of flour on top and gently dust dough. Fold dough from the length about 3–4 times like you would a letter.

6. Cut the dough into strips about 0.3- to 0.5-cm wide, depending on what you prefer. If you are new to this, thicker noodles are easier to handle and cook. Sprinkle a little flour over the noodles and mix to loosen everything. The noodles should not be sticking to each other; if they are, gently separate them and dust with more flour.

7. Bring a large pot of water (at least 2 litres) to a boil over medium heat. Place a large handful of noodles into the boiling water and simmer over medium-low heat for 3–5 minutes. To check doneness, cut one noodle into half. If its cross-section is not white like the dough, it's done.

8. Scoop noodles out with a sieve and shake to drain excess water. Serve hot with your preferred sauce and topping.

NOTES

*   What makes good Chinese noodles is flour with high gluten content. Do not use cake or pastry flours as they are low in gluten.

*   Experiment to find your preferred ratio of wholewheat to all-purpose flour. The more wholewheat flour added, the stronger the nuttiness.

*   Folding from the length makes shorter noodles. For longer noodles, fold from the shorter end. I recommend making shorter noodles as they are easier to cut and handle. To make long noodles, use a sharper knife and keep your hand steady when cutting as the dough is much thicker.

*   These noodles can be stored refrigerated in an airtight container for up to 4 days or portioned and frozen up to 3 months.

Also known as *xian bing*, this is a favourite of mine from my childhood, when I visited my extended family in north China. I would describe this as a love child of savoury pie and pancakes. My family's version is often filled with my mother's signature stir-fried tofu crumbles with aromatic herbs and veggies, encased in a crisp exterior made from wholewheat and plain flour. There are lots of textures and flavours, so this is sure to be a crowd-pleaser. These are also freezable, and thus are good for making ahead and reheating whenever you don't feel like cooking.

savoury chinese pies

Makes about fifteen 7-cm pies

INGREDIENTS

DOUGH

450 g bread or all-
purpose flour
50 g wholewheat flour
250 ml (1 cup) water,
or as needed
5 Tbsp oil for frying, or
as needed

FILLING

250 g firm tofu, about
2–3 blocks, finely
chopped
2 Tbsp oil
5-cm knob ginger,
peeled and minced
2 stalks celery, chopped
$^1/_2$ carrot, chopped
6–7 dried shiitake
mushrooms
15 g dried bean noodles
(*tung hoon*), soaked

SEASONING

2 Tbsp sesame oil
1 Tbsp light soy sauce
2 tsp dark soy sauce
1 Tbsp premium soy
sauce
Sea salt and ground
white pepper, to taste

DIPPING SAUCE

5 Tbsp Chinese black
vinegar
1 Tbsp sesame seeds

METHOD

DOUGH

1. Combine the flours in a large bowl. Adding water a third
    at a time, mix and knead using your hand to form a dough.
    Scrape down the sides and mix well, until there is no more
    flour or residue sticking to the bowl's sides or your fingers.
    If the dough is unable to come together and you still see
    flour after mixing, add more water a little at a time. If the
    dough is too soft and sticky, add more flour.

2. Cover the bowl with a lid or cling film and let sit for at least
    4–6 hours. The dough should feel soft yet retain some
    springiness. That's the most ideal texture.

FILLING

3. Squeeze the tofu gently with a cheesecloth to remove
    excess water. In a frying pan, heat oil over medium heat.
    Sauté the tofu until lightly browned. Mix in ginger and all
    the seasoning ingredients. Set aside to let cool. The tofu
    mixture should be much saltier than what you prefer.

4. In a food processor, blend the celery. Squeeze gently with
    a cheesecloth to remove excess water before and mixing
    together with the tofu.

5. In a food processor, blend carrot, shiitake mushrooms
    and drained bean noodles together. Mix together with tofu
    mixture. You will get a moist filling that binds slightly when
    pressed together. Set aside while preparing the wrappers.

DIPPING SAUCE

6. Mix vinegar and sesame seeds together and serve in
    condiment dishes.

WRAPPING

7. Prepare a large, flat and clean surface to do the rolling. Have a bowl of flour at the side. Lightly flour the surface to prevent dough from sticking. If the dough is too sticky to handle, sprinkle a small handful of flour over and knead it inside the bowl.

8. Cut a third of the dough and keep the remaining portion covered to ensure it doesn't dry out. Roll the dough into a log that is the size and length of a rolling pin. Cut the dough into 5-cm chunks.

9. With one hand on a rolling pin, roll and flatten each dough chunk while rotating it with your other hand, until it becomes a hand-sized round, around 15 cm in diameter. This dough wrapper should be slightly thicker than those for dumplings. The centre portion should be slightly thicker than the outer circumference.

10. Place 2 Tbsp filling in the centre of the wrapper, making sure the filling does not touch the wrapper's edges. Seal the dough around the filling by pinching the edges together, then gently pressing the ball into a puck-like shape, roughly 7 cm in diameter and 1–1.5-cm thick. If there are any holes pinch them to seal. Sprinkle a dash of flour on the top and bottom of each pie to prevent sticking, then place it on a clean surface and flatten gently.

COOKING

11. Heat 5 Tbsp oil in a large frying pan over medium-low heat. Arrange the stuffed pies in the pan, making sure they do not touch each other. Do not overcrowd the pan. Cooking without the use of oil may produce a stronger wheat fragrance, especially if wholewheat flour is used.

12. Flip pies over when the underside starts turning brown. Cook the second side for 30–40 seconds before flipping, then repeat until both sides are golden brown and crispy. The cooking and flipping should be done relatively fast to ensure that the outer crust is crispy while the insides remain soft and juicy.

13. Remove from heat and drain oil on paper towels. Serve hot with dipping sauce.

14. To store, refrigerate cooled pies in an airtight container and keep for up to 5 days. They can be frozen for up to 2 months. Reheat using a microwave, frying pan or toaster oven.

NOTES

- Do not use flours meant for cakes or pastries as they have low gluten content, which will cause the dough to break easily and result in a lack of satisfying chewiness this should have.

- Feel free to increase the ratio of wholewheat flour if you prefer, but it's recommended to add stronger seasoning to the filling as wholewheat flour has quite a strong nuttiness.

- If possible, make the dough 2 days in advance and let sit in the refrigerator. The wrapper's texture will turn out amazingly soft and chewy!

- The veggies can be replaced with others like chives, leek, zucchini, Chinese gourd, water chestnuts, radish, baby bok choy (*xiao bai cai*), Shanghai bok choy, enoki mushrooms, straw mushrooms and more. Avoid veggies that have high water content, like tomatoes. Pickled veggies like pickled radish (*chai poh*), kimchi or pickled Chinese mustard can be a nice addition, but do squeeze them slightly to remove excess water.

- Finding a balanced moisture level for the filling is most important because we don't want a dry or soggy pie. For strong-flavoured veggies like chives and leek, do not squeeze out the water. For veggies like celery and water chestnuts with high-water content, squeeze the water out with a cheesecloth.

- If you have extra filling left, you can make veggie pancakes (page 107). If you have extra dough left, you can make traditional handmade noodles (page 31).

Hokkien mee is an affordable and filling comfort food found at almost every hawker centre. The sound of a wok frying, a whiff of *wok hei* — then finally biting into yellow and white noodles steeped in a rich broth is seriously satisfying. A good Hokkien mee must be fried in a wok, producing quite a bit of smoke. I usually cook this version at home to avoid making the kitchen walls sticky. A claypot is used instead as it's another type of cooking vessel that can impart extra fragrance to the food.

Like the usual Hokkien mee, the stock is very important. To produce an ocean-y umami, two types of seaweed are used together with a source of protein. For textures, I use tofu puffs to soak up the stock, and oyster mushrooms and shiitake to give chewy textural variations.

claypot hokkien mee

Serves 2

INGREDIENTS

STOCK

2 litres (8 cups) water

3 dried shiitake mushrooms

4 pieces dried kelp (kombu)

3 Tbsp dried wakame

2.5-cm knob ginger, peeled and sliced

2 potatoes, peeled and diced

1 tomato, cut into wedges

1/4 cup red lentils or soaked soybeans

1/4 tsp dark soy sauce

1/2 tsp light soy sauce

1 Tbsp fermented soybean paste (*tau cheo*)

HOKKIEN MEE

2 servings of yellow noodles and thick rice noodles, in your preferred proportion

3 Tbsp oil

3 cloves garlic, peeled and minced

2 fried tofu puffs, cut into bite sized pieces

4 blocks firm tofu, broken by hand into smaller pieces

1 large oyster mushroom, sliced

2 handfuls of bean sprouts

3 stalks Chinese chives, cut into 5-cm lengths

1 Tbsp light soy sauce, or to taste

GARNISHES

2 limes, halved

2 Tbsp sambal chilli (see page 26), or to taste

METHOD

STOCK

1. In a soup pot, add water, shiitake, kelp and wakame. Cook over medium-high heat and remove kelp just before the water boils. Add ginger, potato, tomato and lentils or soybeans. Bring to a boil and simmer over medium-low heat for at least 30 minutes.

2. Remove from heat and strain. Season with light soy sauce, dark soy sauce and fermented soybean paste. This should yield 600–800 ml stock.

3. Set aside the cooked shiitake for the noodles.

HOKKIEN MEE

4. Cook the yellow noodles and rice noodles according to packet instructions. Set aside.

5. Heat 2 Tbsp oil in a claypot and add garlic. Fry until light brown.

6. Add yellow noodles, rice noodles, tofu puffs, firm tofu and 125 ml (½ cup) stock. Stir over medium heat for 1 minute until stock is almost absorbed.

7. Add 60 ml (¼ cup) stock, shiitake and oyster mushrooms and bean sprouts. Simmer lightly covered over medium-low heat for 1–2 minutes until bean sprouts are slightly translucent.

8. Add chives, mix everything together, add another 125 ml (½ cup) stock before covering with lid and simmering for 3 minutes.

9. Turn off the heat. Pour 125 ml (½ cup) stock over the cooked noodles, or according to how soupy you prefer the dish. Top with cut limes and sambal chilli.

NOTES

• For the kelp in the stock that was not added to the final dish, you can make kelp pickles, or use it in stir-fries or soups. To make pickles, slice them into strips and marinate in soy sauce, vinegar and spices like star anise or chilli if preferred, and leave overnight in the refrigerator.

• The beauty of homemade Hokkien mee is that you can use whatever noodles you fancy! I recommend thicker noodles as thin noodles will break up after simmering in the broth for some time. Pasta can be a good alternative to Chinese yellow noodles.

• Garlic here can be replaced with preserved Chinese radish (*chai poh*). It gives a wonderful umami while being subtle enough to let other flavours shine.

• Chives add an extra layer of fragrance at the end. It can be replaced with chopped coriander or parsley stem, or ready-to-eat seaweed, which serves the same function with a different flavour profile.

• Gluten-free options: swap yellow noodles with gluten-free pasta and use tamari or liquid aminos to replace soy sauce.

claypot rice

Serves 2

INGREDIENTS
CLAYPOT RICE

1 1/2 Tbsp oil

4 cloves garlic, peeled and minced, or 3-cm knob ginger, peeled and minced)

1 star anise (optional)

2 servings cooked rice

1 large tomato, chopped

3 shiitake mushrooms, sliced

3–5 oyster mushrooms, sliced

2 large napa cabbage leaves, chopped

FRIED TOFU CUBES

2 blocks firm tofu, cubed

1 Tbsp oil

1 Tbsp premium soy sauce

SEASONING

2–3 cubes fermented beancurd (or 2 Tbsp fermented bean paste)

1 Tbsp light soy sauce

1/2 Tbsp dark soy sauce

A few dashes of ground white pepper

80 ml (1/3 cup) stock

1 Tbsp sesame oil, or to taste

GARNISHES

Chopped spring onions or coriander

Sambal or cut chillies

Roasted white sesame seeds

METHOD

1. Fry tofu in a non-stick pan with oil until golden brown. Mix in soy sauce and let tofu absorb it. Remove from heat and set aside.

2. Mixing all the seasoning ingredients in a bowl. Set aside.

3. Heat oil in a claypot over low heat for 1 minute or so. Increase heat to medium-low and add garlic, stirring until fragrant and light brown.

4. Add star anise and rice, stirring to mix well. Pour half of the seasoning over the rice, turn heat to medium-high to bring stock to a boil quickly.

5. Spread tofu, tomato, and mushrooms evenly over the rice.

6. Cover and cook over medium heat for 8–10 minutes. Move to the next step when you smell a smoky char — that's the rice caramelising and starting to stick to the claypot's bottom.

7. Cover tofu and veggies with napa cabbage. Slowly pour over the remaining seasoning in a circular motion to ensure even distribution. Lower heat to medium-low. Cover and cook for another 5–8 minutes, until cabbage is slightly translucent.

8. Turn off the heat and let the claypot sit covered for 5 minutes.

9. Remove cover and serve hot with garnishes of your choice. This is best eaten mixed to enjoy all the flavours together.

NOTES

- Having a layer of charred rice at the bottom is perfectly normal. It provides this claypot rice dish with its signature smokiness.

- If you don't have a claypot, you can use other pots, but try a shorter cooking time as other pots usually have a thinner base.

- Feel free to replace the veggies and mushrooms. Generally, those with high umami content (e.g., white radish, onions, leek, seaweed, celery and portobello mushrooms) work best.

- Other types of protein can be used instead. Chunky types (e.g., seitan, tempeh, vegan meat alternatives) work best here.

- The star anise adds extra fragrance to the rice. You can omit it or try other spices like cinnamon, cloves or black pepper.

- To level up this dish, lightly sauté the mushrooms with a pinch of salt first to bring out more flavours.

- To further boost the flavours, experiment with adding fermented foods like kimchi, miso or even unsweetened pickled plums.

- Instead of fermented bean curd, other fermented bean pastes like miso or gochujang (Korean bean paste) can be used too.

- Gluten-free options: replace soy sauce with tamari or liquid aminos.

- Allium-free options: garlic can be replaced with toon paste, chopped celery, preserved Chinese radish or other preserved vegetables.

This is an easy one-pot dish that uses up leftover rice, turning it into a nourishing and satisfying meal. The trick to making this tasty is to use a strong umami ingredient, which in this case is fermented bean curd with two types of soy sauces . You should also layer your ingredients on top of the rice, so that during the cooking, the juices from the veggies and mushrooms seep into the rice. Thus I usually use vegetables with a higher water content to avoid drying out the pot too much while cooking. A claypot can impart a nice char fragrance when cooked right. To make this a balanced meal, I added tofu. Since rice always pairs best with strong flavours, I avoided using just plain tofu and chose to fry it beforehand.

In Southeast Asia, curry has a special place in our hearts and comes in endless forms. Curry is a type of dish, not a single dish! This version of curry is often found at Chinese food stalls serving a type of fare we call "economic rice". After you've picked a main and chosen the sides, the servers will always ask if you want "gravy". This refers to the curry's gravy which will be ladled on your rice or noodles. I adapted the familiar curry-doused meal so that it can be made at home. To cut down on preparation time, you can make the spice paste in advance and freeze it in portions.

curry tempeh noodles

Serves 2

INGREDIENTS

2 servings of your preferred noodles

2 Tbsp oil

1 small eggplant, cubed

1 tomato, chopped

3–4 pieces tempeh

1–2 Tbsp light soy sauce, or to taste

1 tsp salt

750 ml–1 litre (3–4 cups) water

2–3 stalks long beans

3–4 okra (ladies' fingers)

60 ml (1/4 cup) coconut milk

1–2 Tbsp lemon or lime juice, or to taste

1 sprig coriander, chopped

SPICES

0.5-cm knob ginger, peeled and minced

3 cloves garlic, peeled and minced (or use more ginger)

10–15 curry leaves, or to taste

2–3 dried red chillies, or to taste (optional)

1/3 cup curry powder or 4 Tbsp curry paste

METHOD

1. Cook noodles according to packet instructions and set aside.

2. To fry the spices, heat oil in a pot over medium-low heat. Fry ginger and garlic until lightly browned. Add curry leaves, chillies and curry paste or powder. Mix and fry until fragrant.

3. Add eggplant, tomato, tempeh, 1 Tbsp soy sauce and salt, then mix to coat well with curry spices. Sauté for 2–4 minutes until eggplant is slightly softened.

4. Add water and bring to a boil. Let simmer for 3–5 minutes over low heat.

5. Add the remaining 1 Tbsp soy sauce, long beans, okra and half the coconut milk.

6. Cover pot and cook for 5–8 minutes, until long beans and okra are tender.

7. Add the remaining coconut milk and cooked noodles before removing from the heat.

8. Taste and adjust seasoning with lemon juice and extra soy sauce if preferred. Garnish with coriander and serve hot.

NOTES

- Instead of frying the spices with curry powder or paste, ready-made curry pastes or powders can be used to save time. However, I highly recommend adding curry leaves to a ready-made paste.

- Different veggies or mushrooms can be used for this recipe.

- Pan-frying tempeh or tofu before cooking it in the curry helps to lock in more of the curry flavour. Other proteins you can try in this dish include tofu puffs (*tau pok*), soaked beancurd skin (*tau kee*), seitan (*mian jing*) or canned beans.

- I don't press firm tofu to remove water before use – the Chinese actually don't do that except for some cold dishes. I find that there's no difference in taste and in fact it makes the cooked tofu drier.

- Allium-free option: replace garlic with more ginger, curry leaves, soy sauce and lime or lemon juice.

- Gluten-free option: replace soy sauce with tamari or liquid aminos, and use rice noodles instead.

dough drop soup

Serves 2

INGREDIENTS

DOUGH

¹/₃ cup all-purpose flour
¹/₃ cup wholewheat flour
125 ml (¹/₂ cup) water

SOUP

1 Tbsp oil
1¹/₂ Tbsp minced ginger
³/₄ tsp salt
2 tomatoes, chopped
1 litres (4 cups) stock
2 Tbsp light or premium soy sauce, or to taste
30 g dried bean curd skin, soaked and chopped
3 shiitake mushrooms, finely chopped
8–10 stalks bok choy (or any preferred green leafy vegetable), finely chopped
A dash of ground white pepper

GARNISHES

1 tsp sesame oil
2 stalks spring onion, green part only, finely chopped (optional)
2 sprigs coriander, finely chopped
Chilli oil or paste
Toasted sesame seeds

METHOD

1. To make the soup, heat oil in a medium pot over medium-high heat. Sauté ginger with salt for 20–30 seconds until light brown and fragrant.

2. Add tomatoes and sauté for a minute until saucy.

3. Add stock, soy sauce, bean curd skin and shiitake and bring to a boil. Reduce heat to medium-low and simmer with cover slightly askew.

4. In the meantime, make the dough. Place flours and water in a medium mixing bowl. Using a pair of chopsticks, stir in one direction for 5 minutes until well mixed to get a sticky paste. The longer you stir, the more gluten will develop, making the dough knots even chewier.

5. Tip the bowl to bring the dough towards the edge of the pot. Using a chopstick, push a small bit of dough off the bowl edge and into the boiling soup with a slicing motion. Repeat to use up the dough. Do not pour in large portions at once or you'll end up with huge dough balls. Each dough knot should be bite-sized. Simmer for 1 minute to cook dough knots.

6. Add bok choy and pepper, turn off the heat and mix well. Taste and season with more soy sauce and pepper if preferred.

7. Ladle into bowls and garnish as preferred with sesame oil, spring onion, coriander, chilli oil or paste and sesame seeds.

NOTES

• Another method of making the dough is to put flour in a mixing bowl and drizzle in water bit by bit while stirring with a pair of chopsticks. Keep mixing until you get tiny bits of dough that are loose and not clumped together. You don't have to drop the dough into the boiling soup this way.

• Feel free to add more ingredients. Tofu, seitan, kimchi, other mushrooms or pumpkin will work great.

• Do not cook the dough for too long or it will become tough. The dough knots should be tender and slightly chewy.

My parents are from Northern China so I grew up with memories of *ge da tang*, this gnocchi-like stew eaten as breakfast or a light meal. There are a few different methods to make this. My method is dropping a flour mixture bit by bit into boiling stock or water and cooking until they form little knots, thus the name. The flour thickens the soup base, creating a smooth and thick mouthfeel. This partially wholewheat version is a one-pot dish and extremely easy to make. You can make it with any ingredients you fancy.

Noodles are the ultimate comfort food in many parts of Asia. My favourite is noodle soup, but on hot days, I prefer dry ones. Dry noodles are cooked, drained, tossed in a sauce and topped with whatever you fancy. Highly customisable and easy to pack for lunch boxes.

dry noodles with mushroom mince

Serves 2

INGREDIENTS

150 g plain seitan, torn into strips

2 servings of your preferred noodles

A few drops of sesame oil

2–3 lettuce leaves, chopped

1 sprig coriander, chopped

1 stalk spring onion, green part only, chopped

Chilli flakes to taste

SAUCE

125 ml (¹/₂ cup) stock

1 Tbsp light soy sauce

¹/₂ Tbsp dark soy sauce

1 cube fermented bean curd

1 tsp sugar

¹/₂ Tbsp cooking oil

3 cloves garlic, peeled and minced

0.5-cm knob ginger, peeled and minced

1 tsp salt

³/₄ Tbsp Chinese black vinegar

1 tsp sesame oil

MUSHROOM MINCE

1 Tbsp oil

5-cm stalk leek, finely chopped

6 shiitake mushrooms (or your preferred mushrooms), about 140 g, finely chopped

1 Tbsp light or premium soy sauce

3–4 Tbsp water or stock

SOUP

600 ml stock

4 stalks spring onion or 4 sprigs coriander, chopped

¹/₂ tsp salt, or to taste

METHOD

1. To make the sauce, place stock, both soy sauces, fermented bean curd and sugar in a mixing bowl. Mix until combined. Set aside.

2. Heat cooking oil over medium-low heat in a saucepan. Sauté garlic and ginger with salt for a minute or until lightly browned and fragrant. Add seitan strips and sauté for a couple of minutes until lightly browned. Remove seitan strips and set aside. To the sautéed garlic and ginger, add the stock mixture, stirring to dissolve the fermented bean curd. Bring to a gentle boil, then remove from heat and mix in black vinegar and sesame oil. This makes about 250 ml. Set aside.

3. To make the mushroom mince, start by heating oil in a frying pan over medium heat. Add leek and sauté for 40–60 seconds until slightly translucent and fragrant.

4. Add mushrooms and soy sauce, then sauté until mushrooms shrink to almost half their size. Add 2 Tbsp stock, lower heat to medium-low and let it reduce. The mushrooms should be moist, glistening and slightly sticky. If not, add 1 Tbsp stock at a time and reduce until they are. Set aside.

5. Cook noodles according to packet instructions. Drain and add a few drops of sesame oil and mix well to coat. Set aside.

6. To make the soup, bring stock to a boil. Remove from heat, season with salt to taste and add spring onions or coriander.

7. To assemble, pour sauce over noodles and mix well. Portion into bowls and arrange lettuce leaves on the side. Top with mushroom mince, seitan strips, coriander or spring onions, and chilli flakes. Serve warm with soup.

NOTES

*   Seitan strips can be replaced with other toppings such as cooked chickpeas, fried tempeh, tofu puffs and nuts.

*   Fermented beancurd adds an extra layer of umami and makes the sauce slightly creamier. It can be replaced with 1 heaping Tbsp white miso, or simply omit and add more soy sauce and black vinegar to taste.

*   Allium-free options: The garlic in the sauce can be omitted with more ginger added in place. The leek in the mushroom mince can be replaced with finely chopped celery or 1¹/₂ Tbsp toon paste to add a base fragrance to the mince.

*   Gluten-free options: use tofu or tempeh instead of seitan. Swap the soy sauce for tamari or liquid aminos.

*   When I cook noodles that need to be set aside for later, I always add a bit of oil after draining. It prevents the noodles from sticking as they cool.

*   Because the noodles are meant to taste heavier, the soup is kept light. Feel free to omit the soup if you like and pair with your favourite drink instead.

herbal soy sauce noodles

Serves 2

INGREDIENTS

2 servings of your preferred noodles

1¹/₂ Tbsp cooking oil

0.5-cm knob ginger, peeled and minced

6 cloves garlic, peeled, crushed and roughly chopped

2–3 star anise

4–5 white peppercorns

1 stick cinnamon

2 Tbsp + 2 Tbsp premium soy sauce

2 litres (8 cups) water or stock

2 pieces *danggui* (Chinese angelica root), optional

8 dried goji berries, optional

2 red dates, optional

6–8 tofu puffs

4–6 sheets dried bean curd skin

4–6 shiitake mushrooms, stems removed, halved

4–6 wood's ear fungus

1 medium king oyster mushroom, thinly sliced

125 ml (¹/₂ cup) unsweetened soy or oat milk

GARNISHES

1 stalk spring onion or coriander, chopped (optional)

1 tsp white sesame seeds

METHOD

1. Cook noodles according to packet instructions and set aside.

2. Heat oil in a pot over medium-low heat for about 2 minutes before adding ginger and garlic and frying until fragrant.

3. Add star anise, peppercorns and cinnamon, then fry until fragrant.

4. Add 2 Tbsp soy sauce, then cook until liquid is almost reduced. This caramelises the soy sauce.

5. Add water or stock and bring to a boil.

6. If using, add *danggui*, goji berries and red dates. Add another 2 Tbsp soy sauce, tofu puffs, bean curd skin and mushrooms. Cover and simmer over medium-low for 15–20 minutes.

7. Remove from heat and add noodles and soy milk. Taste and add more pepper and soy sauce if preferred.

8. Garnish with spring onions or coriander and sesame seeds. Serve hot.

NOTES

- Other ingredients that you can use are: any type of mushroom, firm tofu, greens like bok choy, and seitan chunks.

- Stock is recommended to make a tastier soup. Use a light stock to let the soy sauce and spice flavours shine.

- The unsweetened soy milk adds body and smoothness to the soup. It also increases protein content, which helps boost the umami level. Other non-dairy milks like oat and almond can be used too, but never use sweetened or flavoured ones in savoury dishes.

- As plant milks may separate under heat, I usually let the portion needed sit at room temperature before I start preparing the dish. This reduces the temperature gap.

- Allium-free options: the garlic can be omitted and replaced with more ginger and pepper. Adding some chopped celery gives an additional layer of fragrance to the soup. Spring onion can be replaced with chopped coriander for garnishing.

- Gluten-free options: swap soy sauce for tamari or liquid aminos.

This nourishing one-pot is inspired by *bak kut teh*, a local favourite which literally translates to "pork bone tea" in Hokkien. It is a garlicky, peppery and sometimes herbal pork soup that has variations among various Chinese dialect groups. Here's the plant-based version that's also nourishing and familiar. The secret ingredient is unsweetened soy milk, which adds a creamy mouthfeel to the soup while boosting savouriness. Plant milks may separate if subjected to sudden high heat, so remove your soy milk from the refrigerator and set aside the portion needed earlier.

Do you like curry but dislike spicy food? Japanese curry is for you. It's known to be smoother, milder and sweeter than other curries while still packing lots of appetite-inducing flavours. The first time I made this curry was in Hokkaido, using only Hokkaido vegetables and curry powder. It was a simple recipe but it tasted so amazing because Hokkaido produce is top-notch. I've realised that most ready-made curry roux are full of ingredients that are hard to pronounce, thus I made a version that uses only natural spices and plants. The natural starchy thickener here is pumpkin. Top this smooth curry on tender udon noodles or rice and eat to your heart's content!

japanese pumpkin curry udon

Serves 2

INGREDIENTS

2 servings of udon noodles

1½ Tbsp oil

1 medium onion, peeled and finely chopped

1 tsp salt

1 heaping Tbsp Japanese curry powder

300 g *kabocha* (Japanese pumpkin), skin removed, finely diced

1 medium carrot, peeled and cubed

2 litres (8 cups) water or stock

1½ Tbsp regular soy sauce

1 tsp lemon or lime juice (optional)

TO SERVE

1 stalk spring onion, chopped finely

2 lentil potato croquettes (see page 97)

METHOD

1. Cook udon according to packet instructions. Drain and set aside.

2. In a large pot, heat oil over medium-low heat. Add onion and salt and sauté until slightly translucent. Add curry powder and mix quickly to distribute evenly.

3. Add *kabocha* and carrots, then sauté for 3–5 minutes until slightly darkened and well coated with curry powder. Add water or stock. Bring to a boil before reducing the heat to medium-low and simmering with cover slightly askew for 30–40 minutes, until *kabocha* is soft. Periodically use a spatula to scrape the bottom and check if the curry is sticking. If it is, stir and lower the heat to prevent burning.

4. Using a fork and spoon, carefully mash the *kabocha* and stir into the curry. For best results, the *kabocha* should be dissolved into the curry, making it thicker. Add soy sauce, check if carrots are done and then adjust seasoning with more salt, soy sauce, curry powder or lemon juice. It should be slightly saltier than what you prefer.

5. To serve, portion udon into bowls. Ladle curry over, top with spring onion and croquettes as preferred.

NOTES

- You can replace udon with rice or bread, or simply have the curry as it is. If you are not having the curry with a main, I suggest reducing the salt to ½ tsp.

- Any type of curry powder can work with this recipe, but Japanese-style works the best because the spice blend is on the gentler side. It will produce a more balanced flavour that brings out the natural sweetness of the vegetables. If you don't have it, you can use other curry powders but reduce amount to slightly more than ½ Tbsp.

- Pumpkin can be replaced with potato or sweet potato; its purpose is to naturally sweeten and thicken the curry. Feel free to add other vegetables or ingredients.

- If you don't have time to make lentil croquettes, you can add tofu, tempeh or beans for protein to make this a complete and filling meal. For tofu and tempeh, pan-fry before topping the curry with it for best flavour. If you can make the croquettes, I highly recommend it as it goes best with this curry. The breadcrumb exterior soaks up the curry perfectly.

- Allium-free options: the onion can be replaced with finely chopped celery and minced ginger. 1 Tbsp toon paste can also add some onion-like flavour.

- Gluten-free options: use thick rice noodles or gluten-free udon.

kway chap

Serves 2

INGREDIENTS

$1/2$ cup raw peanuts (or cashews)

$1/4$ cup pinto beans, soaked overnight and drained (other larger beans with skin like navy beans or chickpeas work well too)

$1/4$ cup red lentils or similar small lentils

8 dried shiitake mushrooms, soaked for at least 30 minutes

4–6 pieces black fungus

2 blocks firm tofu

300 g plain seitan

40 g Chinese pickled mustard (optional but highly recommended)

4–6 sheets dried bean curd skin (*yuba*), roughly 30g, soaked until soft

4 pieces tofu puffs (*tau pok*)

2 sprigs coriander, chopped

GRAVY (*CHAP*)

1 Tbsp oil

1 Tbsp black peppercorns

1 stick cinnamon

$1/2$ Tbsp five-spice powder

2.5 litres (10 cups) water, or more as needed

5 cloves garlic, peeled and crushed

40 g ginger, roughly a 7-cm knob, peeled and sliced

1 Tbsp Chinese black vinegar

3 Tbsp dark soy sauce

6 Tbsp premium soy sauce, or to taste

2 Tbsp sugar, or to taste

RICE NOODLES(*KWAY*)

2 servings of rice noodle sheets or flat rice noodles

500–750 ml (2–3 cups) water, or more as needed

METHOD

1. To make the gravy, heat oil in a stock pot over medium heat and add peppercorns, cinnamon and five-spice powder. Fry until fragrant, then add the water and bring to a boil.

2. Add garlic, ginger, vinegar, soy sauces and sugar. Boil for 2 minutes.

3. Add peanuts, beans, lentils, shiitake, black fungus, firm tofu, seitan, pickled mustard and bean curd skin, and simmer over low heat for 1–1.5 hours until the liquid is reduced by almost half. Add tofu puffs and cook for another 20–30 minutes. If the stock starts to dry out, add 60 ml ($1/4$ cup) water to prevent this. When it's done, turn off the heat, cover and set aside to rest for 30 minutes.

4. Blanch rice noodles, drain and portion into bowls. If you are using rice sheets, be sure to cut them first. Strain the stock and set aside ingredients. Transfer about 1 litre (4 cups) stock (or more if needed) into another pot. Add water and bring to a boil. Taste soup and adjust seasoning with some soy sauce if preferred. Ladle over noodles and garnish with chopped coriander if preferred.

5. To serve, slice shiitake, firm tofu blocks, tofu puffs, bean curd skin and pickled mustard into bite-sized pieces. Arrange braised ingredients on 2 plates. Place pickled mustard, cooked peanuts and pinto beans on the side. Drizzle 60 ml ($1/4$ cup) braising stock or more over and serve.

6. Leftover braised items can be refrigerated for up to 5 days or frozen.

NOTES

- If you don't have access to ready-made rice roll sheets (*chee cheong fun*), you can use any other type of rice noodles. The braised side dish goes fantastic with plain rice too!

- Lentils aren't a traditional *kway chap* ingredient. Here, it will dissolve after cooking, thickening and improving umami flavour in the soup.

- Chinese vinegar also isn't a traditional ingredient, but it helps tenderise the proteins and add a bit more umami to the soup.

- Don't throw away excess braising stock because its packed with so much flavour. Just add stock or water to it, as you would in making the soup for *kway chap*, then add noodles and other toppings for a quick meal. It can even be used as a topping for rice, porridge or base sauce for dry noodles.

- If you can find Chinese pickled mustard (*mei cai*), I highly recommend adding it as it boosts the savouriness of the stock.

- Allium-free options: the garlic can replaced with more chopped celery and ginger, spices and pickled vegetables.

- Gluten-free options: swap the soy sauce for tamari or liquid aminos, and use rice or balsamic vinegar instead of Chinese vinegar.

Kway chap is another well-loved classic found in Singapore's hawker centres. The name comes from the dish's two parts: flat and broad rice sheets (the *kway*) in a soup, accompanied by a side dish of braised offal and other meat ingredients in a rich soy sauce based gravy (the *chap*). In this version, we will use beans, nuts, mushrooms, seitan and various types of soy-based ingredients for a wholesome, slurp-worthy dish.

Nasi means "rice", while *lemak* means "rich". So *nasi lemak* refers to the fluffy rice cooked in rich coconut milk. In this dish, the rice gets paired with a bold, spicy chilli paste (sambal chilli), egg (replaced with tofu here), fried peanuts and anchovies (vegetarian versions use crunchy mushroom stems), and sliced cucumber and tomato. Lots of textures going on! Some add a serving of rendang (dry curry) to make it a more filling meal. Here I'll share the basic version. You can refer to page 88 for my tempeh rendang recipe.

The soul of this dish is undoubtedly the sambal. We will use homemade sambal chilli as a base and liven it up even more with onions and tamarind, as well as a bit of wakame for a familiar ocean-y flavour (non-vegan sambal sometimes has shrimp). When a good sambal gets mixed with freshly cooked coconut rice, you're having an experience, not just tasting it!

nasi lemak

Serves 2

INGREDIENTS

NASI LEMAK

1 cup rice, rinsed

375 ml (1 1/2 cups) water

125 ml (1/2 cup) coconut milk

A pinch of salt

3 pandan leaves, tied into knots

1 stalk lemongrass, halved

CRISPY RICE NOODLES

125 ml (1/2 cup) oil, or as needed

1 small bunch dried rice noodles, cut into roughly 1-cm lengths

SAMBAL CHILLI

1 Tbsp oil

1/2 onion, peeled and chopped

1 Tbsp dried wakame, crushed (optional)

1/3 cup vegan sambal chilli (see page 26)

1 heaping scoop tamarind paste, about the size of a table tennis ball, soaked in warm water

ACCOMPANIMENTS

3 Tbsp oil

1/4 cup peanuts

2 blocks firm tofu, cut into bite-sized cubes

1 tsp light or regular soy sauce

1/2 cucumber, sliced

1/2 tomato, sliced

METHOD

1. Place rice in a pot. Add water, coconut milk, salt, pandan leaves and lemongrass. The liquid should cover the rice completely, with about 4–5 cm to spare.

2. Bring to a boil, then reduce the heat to low. Cover and cook for 15–20 minutes until the cooking liquid is fully absorbed and holes appear on the surface. Turn off the heat, keep covered and set aside for 10 minutes before serving.

3. For the crispy rice noodles, heat oil in a frying pan. Take a few longer noodle pieces in your hand and dip just the ends in the oil. If they puff up, the oil is hot enough. With a spatula at the ready, gently drop handfuls of noodles into the oil. When they bloom, which should be in a few seconds, quickly flip them once, then transfer onto paper towels to drain and set aside. Do not cook for more than a few seconds to avoid burning.

4. For the sambal chilli, heat oil in a frying pan or wok. Add onion and wakame, and sauté until onion is translucent. Add sambal, then sauté for 10–15 seconds until fragrant. Add tamarind juice, then simmer over low heat until mixture is reduced and thickened. Remove from heat and set aside.

5. Heat 2 Tbsp oil in a frying pan over medium-high heat. Fry peanuts until brown, transfer to drain on paper towels and set aside. Ensure there are no crumbs in your pan to avoid burnt bits.

6. By now, the oil should have absorbed the fragrance of the peanuts. Add the remaining oil and fry tofu pieces until golden brown on one side. Drizzle soy sauce over tofu, flip and fry until the other side is golden brown. Remove from heat and drain on paper towels.

7. To assemble, place rice in the centre of a plate. Arrange tofu, peanuts, crispy rice noodles, sliced cucumbers and tomatoes on the side. Serve hot with sambal chilli.

NOTES

- Nasi lemak is best served on a banana leaf, as it imparts extra fragrance to the dish. It also pairs well with a cup of teh tarik (page 128).

- You can use any sambal you like. In a dish where the sambal is the star, I prefer to refresh the chilled sambal by cooking it a bit first.

- If you have black salt, sprinkle it over the fried tofu for an extra egg-like umami flavour.

- In Singapore, vegan nasi lemak usually comes with crispy mushroom stems in place of anchovies. But as this option may not be widely available, I used common pantry ingredients to create something with a similar crispiness. The crispy rice noodles are puffy and absorb the sambal well!

- Allium-free option: the onion can be replaced with 2 Tbsp toon paste.

- Gluten-free options: swap the soy sauce for tamari or liquid aminos.

okonomiyaki

Makes 3 medium pancakes

INGREDIENTS
BATTER

2 pieces dried kelp (kombu)

4 dried shiitake mushrooms

800 ml (3¼ cups) water, at room temperature

1 cup flour, sifted

½ tsp salt

7.5-cm Chinese mountain yam, grated

1 tsp rice or apple cider vinegar

80 ml (⅓ cup) unsweetened soy milk

½ tsp light soy sauce

¼ tsp baking powder

2 Tbsp oil

FILLING

½ head medium cabbage, finely chopped

1 tomato, finely chopped

4 shiitake mushrooms (from making batter), finely chopped

¼ stalk leek, finely chopped

Slices of marinated tofu or tempeh, or your preferred protein

METHOD
OKONOMIYAKI

1. To make stock for the batter, soak kelp and shiitake in 800 ml water for at least 1 hour.

2. Remove kelp and shiitake, then cut the shiitake into thin strips and set aside. Reserve soaking liquid as stock. The kelp can be added to other recipes like clear soups.

3. In a large mixing bowl, mix flour and salt. Add mountain yam and 180 ml (¾ cup) stock and mix well.

4. Mix in vinegar, soy milk, soy sauce and baking powder until just combined. Cover and refrigerate for at least 1 hour.

5. Add chopped vegetables and mushrooms a third at a time, mixing well before adding the next portion. The batter should be sticky and thick with visible air bubbles.

6. Heat oil in a non-stick pan. When the oil is hot, pour a third of the batter into the pan. Use spatulas to gently press the batter into a round shape. Press slices of tofu or tempeh on top of the batter.

7. On medium-low heat, cook covered for 3–4 minutes until browned on the bottom. Check by lifting up the pancake with one spatula. If it starts breaking when lifted or the bottom is still pale, it's not ready yet.

8. When the first side is browned, use 2 spatulas to flip the pancake and cook the other side. Cook until browned, then transfer to a plate. Repeat to make more pancakes until the batter is used up.

9. Top with okonomiyaki sauce, mayonnaise, *aonori*, spring onions and other toppings you like. Serve hot.

TOPPINGS

Japanese mayonnaise (see page 25)

Vegan okonomiyaki sauce (see method)

Chopped spring onions (optional)

Aonori (*aosa* / green laver) or similar seaweed flakes

Other topping ideas: Chilli sauce, fried onions, soy floss, black pepper, chilli flakes, sesame seeds, etc

OKONOMIYAKI SAUCE

1/4 cup ketchup

1 tsp tamarind paste (or use 1 tsp lime or lemon juice mixed with 1 tsp brown sugar; or mash 1 sweet pickled plum and mix in 1 tsp water, then strain, using only the liquid.)

1 1/2 Tbsp light or regular soy sauce

1 Tbsp dark soy sauce

1 tsp rice or apple cider vinegar

A dash of chilli sauce, to taste

A small pinch of ground clove or five-spice powder (optional but recommended)

2 Tbsp maple syrup or light-flavoured syrup sweetener

1 tsp cornstarch

OKONOMIYAKI SAUCE

10. In a mixing bowl, whisk all the ingredients together.

11. Transfer to a pot, bring to a gentle boil and stir while simmering until syrup dissolves.

12. Taste and adjust seasoning accordingly. It should be savoury, tangy and sweet with fruity undertones. The texture should be like that of oyster sauce: smooth and slightly thick, just enough to spread easily. This makes about 125 ml (1/2 cup).

NOTES

- To avoid pushing out air out of the batter, do not over mix it. Stop when everything is just combined.
- A good okonomiyaki has tempura bits. It helps make the batter fluffier. If you can get tempura bits, I highly recommend adding 80 ml (1/3 cup) to the batter. Note that not all types are plant-based.
- The vegetables in the filling can be replaced with other vegetables.
- Start by making smaller pancakes as they are easier to flip. Don't hesitate when you're flipping them and do it with one quick action.
- If you have kombu stock powder, I highly recommend adding a teaspoonful into the batter and sauce. It brings out a lot more umami!
- Allium-free options: swap the leek in the filling with chopped chillies, ginger or toon sauce.

12

Okonomiyaki is a customisable savoury pancake — *okonomi* means "as you like" and yaki means "fried" or "stir-fried". It's popular all across Japan but especially well known in Osaka and Hiroshima, where the two main styles of okonomiyaki are from. The ingredients in Osaka style are mixed, while in the Hiroshima style they are layered. This is a plant-based take on Osaka's version. The tender and slightly gooey pancake usually contains egg in the batter, but here we will use a combination of baking powder, vinegar, unsweetened soy milk and grated Chinese mountain yam to achieve the same texture.

Traditional *okonomiyaki* already contains Chinese mountain yam to lift the batter. It's naturally sticky and smooth without flavour – a fantastic egg replacement in certain applications. The batter also has baking powder — here we are combining it with vinegar to produce air bubbles and prevents a dense or doughy pancake. You can use any type of vinegar with a light flavour, like rice, apple cider or distilled vinegar. Soy milk adds protein and moisture, which also helps yield a light and moist texture.

Okonomiyaki sauce is similar to Worcestershire sauce but has added tang, sweetness and savouriness. Since most people may not have access to vegan Worcestershire sauce or *okonomi* sauce, I came up with this simple recipe using common ingredients in an Asian pantry.

A savoury, stew-like dish perfect for cold or rainy weather. *Mee hoon kway* is Hokkien term for a type flat hand-torn noodles. You can make them from scratch by following the handmade noodles recipe (page 31) and tearing the dough into pieces instead of cutting it into long noodles. With a natural creamy texture and slightly sweet aftertaste thanks to the pumpkin, the soup is great for kids. Eating this with a spoon is highly recommended!

pumpkin miso
mee hoon kway

Makes 2 servings

INGREDIENTS

1¹/₂ Tbsp cooking oil

2 slices pumpkin, around 600 g, skin removed, cut into small cubes

2 ripe medium tomatoes

A pinch of salt

¹/₃ cup split red lentils, soaked for 30 minutes

2 litres (8 cups) stock or water

6–8 shiitake mushrooms, sliced

2 servings of *mee hoon kway* (see page 31)

1 heaping Tbsp white miso

GARNISHES

Spring onion or coriander, chopped, to taste

Ground white pepper, to taste

METHOD

1. In a pot, heat oil over medium-low heat. Add pumpkin, tomatoes and salt, and sauté for 30 seconds.

2. Place lentils together with water or stock in a pot and bring to a boil. With cover set slightly askew, cook over medium-low heat for 30 minutes, or until lentils are soft.

3. Using a fork or masher, mash the pumpkin until it dissolves into the soup.

4. Add mushrooms and *mee hoon kway*. Reduce the heat and add more stock or water if there's not enough soup to just cover the noodles and mushrooms.

5. Cook for 2–4 minutes until *mee hoon kway* reaches desired softness.

6. Turn off the heat, then dissolve miso into the stew.

7. Taste and adjust seasoning, adding more miso if preferred. Garnish to taste and serve hot.

NOTES

- Instead of pumpkin, you can use sweet potato or squash, or more tomatoes.
- *Mee hoon kway* can be replaced with any other noodles.
- This can also be a stew on its own without the noodles.
- Gluten-free option: swap *mee hoon kway* with gluten-free pasta.

Tearing *mee hoon kway* by hand

savoury quinoa and brown rice porridge

Serves 2

INGREDIENTS
PORRIDGE

1 tsp oil

2 cloves garlic, peeled and minced

1-cm knob ginger, peeled and minced

4–5 shiitake mushrooms, chopped

1/4 cup white quinoa

1 cup cooked brown rice

2.25 litres (9 cups) stock

4–6 stalks mild-flavoured green vegetables (Chinese broccoli, *xiao bai cai*, bok choy, *cai xin*, etc.), finely chopped

2 Tbsp light soy sauce

1/2 tsp ground white pepper

TO SERVE

Spring onions, thinly sliced

Fried onions or garlic

Coriander, chopped

Roasted peanuts

Roasted sesame seeds

Soy sauce

Sesame oil

Chilli paste

Fermented bean curd

METHOD

1. Heat oil in a large, heavy pot over medium heat. Sauté garlic, ginger and mushrooms until mushrooms are softened.

2. Add quinoa, rice and stock, and bring to a boil. Reduce to a simmer and cook, stirring occasionally to prevent the rice from sticking to the bottom. If a thinner consistency is desired, add more stock as needed.

3. After 1 hour, stir in the greens. Continue simmering for another 30 minutes or so until it reaches the consistency of porridge.

4. Season to taste with salt or soy sauce and pepper. Serve hot with garnishes and condiments of your choice.

5. This may be refrigerated for up to 4 days, but it will thicken. Add more water or stock when reheating.

NOTES

- White quinoa works best as tricolour quinoa tends to have inconsistent textures after cooking.

- This is a basic recipe. The porridge itself has a mild flavour and pairs with strong umami and savoury condiments and sides. Feel free to top this off with anything you fancy. My favourite combination is soy sauce, sesame oil, fermented bean curd and coriander. Ingredients like pickled mustard greens (*suan cai*), pickled Chinese mustard (*mei cai*), marmite or even kimchi or umeboshi will go well with this.

- Allium-free options: garlic can replaced with minced mushrooms or more ginger.

- Gluten-free options: swap the soy sauce for tamari or liquid aminos.

Porridge is the ultimate comfort food for many Chinese. Said to be easily digested, it's the food our mothers or grandmothers always make when we are sick. In my house, we often use quinoa and brown rice to make it more nutritious with more protein. I personally love to add a colourful variety of savoury veggies, mushrooms and condiments. This is also a fantastic way to use up leftover rice. In fact, the best porridge is made from overnight rice.

There are two types of people in the world: people who love sweet breakfasts and people who can't start the day without a savoury one. I am the latter. The deep purple of beetroot is surely a bright way to start the day for savoury breakfast lovers. I cook this sometimes when I get tired of bread or have no more leftover rice for rice porridge. It's one-pot, easy and versatile. Sweet breakfast lovers, don't worry, you can make this as a meal any time of the day. Also as this is easy to chew and has a natural sweetness, this is a fantastic way to get children to eat their veggies.

savoury beetroot oatmeal porridge

Serves 2

INGREDIENTS

1 Tbsp oil

4 shiitake mushrooms, diced

A pinch of salt

$^3/_4$ medium beetroot, peeled and diced

2 Tbsp regular or premium soy sauce

1.2 litres (4 $^3/_4$ cups) stock or water

1 cup baby oats

A few dashes of ground white pepper

GARNISHES

1 Tbsp sesame oil

1 stalk spring onion, green part only, finely chopped

1 sprig coriander or 1 stalk spring onion, finely chopped

Fried garlic or onions

METHOD

1. Heat oil in a pot over medium-low heat. Add shiitake with a pinch of salt and sauté until they shrink slightly.

2. Add beetroot and mix well with shiitake. Add 1 Tbsp soy sauce, let it simmer and reduce to half. Add water or stock, bring to a boil and simmer for 15–20 minutes, until beetroot is soft. Mix in the remaining soy sauce.

3. Bring heat down to low and carefully add in baby oats while stirring. Let it simmer for 5–10 minutes, stirring until oats are cooked and a sticky, porridge-like texture is achieved. Add extra water or stock if any oats stick to the bottom of the pot, or if the porridge is getting too thick.

4. Remove from heat, taste and adjust seasoning with pepper and salt. Serve in bowls and top with garnishes as preferred.

NOTES

- This is a very versatile recipe. Beetroot can be substituted with pumpkin, squash, sweet potato, tomato — anything that cooks to a paste-like consistency, can give a nice colour and has a natural subtle sweetness. Shiitake here is used for its enriching woody flavour and meaty texture, though you can substitute with a strong-flavoured item like portobello, porcini or button mushrooms, or leek, onions or garlic.

- You can also replace oats with cooked rice or other cook grains to make other types of porridge.

- Adding only half of the soy sauce first and reducing it will concentrate it and bring out even more umami. Since the ingredients here are simple, I think it is quite important to do this to make the porridge tasty.

- Gluten-free options: swap the soy sauce for tamari or liquid aminos, and use gluten-free oats.

tom yum fried quinoa

Serves 2

INGREDIENTS

1 Tbsp + 1^1/$_2$ Tbsp oil

200 g soft tofu

A pinch of salt

A pinch of ground turmeric (optional)

3 kaffir lime leaves

3 cloves garlic, peeled and minced

1^1/$_2$ Tbsp vegan tom yum paste, or to taste

1 cup oyster mushrooms, about 10, chopped

2 cups cooked white quinoa

1 Tbsp regular or premium soy sauce, or to taste

^{1}/$_3$ cup corn, carrot and peas mix

GARNISHES

1 stalk spring onion (green part only), chopped, (optional)

1 lime, halved

1 tsp roasted white sesame seeds

METHOD

1. Heat 1 Tbsp oil in a pan over medium heat. Add tofu, salt and turmeric. Break tofu using a spatula and scramble until you don't see much liquid in the pan and tofu is evenly yellow. Transfer to a bowl and set aside.

2. Using your hand, crush lime leaves to release their fragrance. Add 1½ Tbsp oil to a wok, toss in leaves, garlic with tom yum paste and sauté for 5–10 seconds over medium-low heat until fragrant.

3. Add oyster mushrooms and quinoa, tossing quickly to mix well with tom yum paste.

4. Add soy sauce and mixed vegetables, stirring quickly until everything is coated evenly with tom yum paste. Add scrambled tofu and mix well.

5. Remove from heat, taste and adjust seasoning with more soy sauce if needed. Serve hot with garnishes as preferred.

NOTES

*   Before cooking, it's best to taste the tom yum paste first for its saltiness so that you can adjust the seasoning according to what you prefer.
*   Tom yum paste can be replaced with any spice paste or powder.
*   Allium-free options: garlic can be replaced with 2 Tbsp toon paste. The onion-like flavour goes well with tom yum too. In fact, toon fried rice (香椿炒饭) is a popular item in Chinese vegetarian eateries! Spring onion for garnishing can be replaced with chopped coriander.
*   Gluten-free options: swap the soy sauce for tamari or liquid aminos.

I've always found quinoa a bit difficult to use in Asian cuisine, because it's not as fragrant or fluffy as rice. However it's a superfood and a complete protein, so I found a way to enjoy it — with bold, spicy flavours that are familiar and exciting. White quinoa works best with this recipe as it can be cooked to a decently fluffy texture. For the veggies and mushroom here, feel free to replace with anything you like. If you can't find vegan tom yum paste near you, substitute with your favourite curry paste or sauce.

My family's annual Chinese New Year tradition is Shandong-style dumplings made from scratch. This recipe has been used since my grandmother's generation and refined over many years. The process is so complex that the whole family needs to be involved. My father prepares and kneads the dough, my mother makes the filling, and I help with the wrapping. They only let me start wrapping when I was a bit older, around age 12 or so, after observing the process many times. Over time, and with practice, you'll get the hang of the nuances.

According to my grandmother, the main secret to making good vegan dumplings is stir-frying the tofu with ginger and a combination of soy sauces. She has said that when this is done right, it will taste like chicken. Knowing how to process the vegetables is important too. Veggies, unlike meat, release a lot of water when cooked. If there is too much water, it will dilute the flavours of the filling. Lastly, the wrapper is made one by one to ensure a balanced texture. Each wrapper is slightly thicker in the middle to prevent the dumpling from bursting at the belly while cooking, and to avoid making the top of the dumpling too thick when pinched. Thus all the steps in this recipe are important — don't skip any!

When we make dumplings for reunion dinner, we eat only dumplings and have extras to pan-fry for the next day's breakfast! Each adult can eat about 20 to 30 of these, which is why this recipe has a large yield. Feel free to half it.

traditional dumplings

Makes around 120 dumplings

INGREDIENTS

DOUGH

1 kg all-purpose flour
550 ml (2 ¼ cups) water

FILLING

800 g napa cabbage

1 tsp salt

8 dried shiitake mushrooms, soaked and rinsed

1 stalk Japanese scallion, cut into sections

2 Tbsp sesame oil

2 tsp sea salt, or to taste

2 tsp ground white pepper, or to taste

4 Tbsp cooking oil, preferably soybean or peanut oil

8 blocks firm tofu, finely chopped

0.5-cm knob ginger, peeled and finely chopped

1 Tbsp light soy sauce

2 tsp dark soy sauce

1 Tbsp premium soy sauce

METHOD

1. Sift flour into a large bowl. Add a third of the water at a time, mixing to incorporate and kneading the mixture into a dough. Scrape down the sides and mix well, until there is no more flour or residue sticking to the bowl's sides or your fingers. This is the most ideal texture.

2. Cover the bowl with a lid or plastic wrap and let it sit for at least 1 hour. The dough will reach its most ideal texture after 4–6 hours, when it feels soft while maintaining some springiness.

3. Blend cabbage into fine pieces using a food processor. Add salt and mix well. Place in a cheesecloth and squeeze out liquid from cabbage, but retain some moisture to maintain the freshness of the cabbage.

4. Place in a food processor with soaked shiitake and blend until fine. Transfer to a bowl and add scallion to blended mixture. Add sesame oil and mix well before seasoning with sea salt and pepper. Set aside.

5. Add cooking oil to a large pan over medium heat. Add tofu and stir-fry for 3–4 minutes, until more than half of its liquid has evaporated. Stir in the mashed ginger and soy sauces, then cook over high heat briefly before letting the tofu cool. Taste to check that it is very savoury and much saltier than what you prefer. That's expected, as we will be mixing it with other ingredients.

6. When stir-fried tofu is cooled, mix in cabbage mixture. Taste to make sure it is saltier than preferred, adding more salt and pepper if needed.

7. Prepare a large, flat and clean surface to do the rolling. Have a bowl of flour on the side. Lightly flour the surface to prevent dough from sticking.

8. Cut a portion of dough from the main chunk and cover the remaining dough with a cloth to keep it from drying out.

9. Roll dough portion into a log similar to the size and length of a rolling pin. Cut dough log into smaller portions equivalent to the size of glutinous rice balls. Flatten each piece slightly with your hand.

10. With a rolling pin beneath one hand, roll and flatten each small portion of dough while rotating it with your other hand until you obtain a flat round wrapper. The outer circumference should be about 0.2–0.3-mm thick. The centre should be slightly thicker than the edges.

11. To wrap, lightly flour your hands before placing a wrapper on one hand. Place 1 tsp filling in the centre, and fold the wrapper in half with the other hand. Firmly pinch where the 2 edges meet at the top to seal, leaving the two ends open. To make a nice pattern, pinch to seal at the midpoint of the sealed top and each open end. Now you will get 4 small openings — pinch them all to seal.

12. Dust the bottom of each dumpling with flour to prevent sticking and place on a clean surface. Repeat until the dough is used up.

13. To cook, place a pot of water over high heat and slip in the dumplings. Make sure they do not stick to the sides of the pot, and avoid overcrowding the pot. When the water comes to a boil, add a bowl of room-temperature water to reduce its temperature. Let the water come to a boil again.

DIPPING SAUCE

Coriander, finely chopped

Ginger, peeled and cut into matchsticks

2 Tbsp cut chillies or chilli sauce

4 cloves garlic, peeled and minced (optional)

8 Tbsp light soy sauce

5 Tbsp Chinese black vinegar

2 Tbsp sesame oil

14. When the water comes to a boil again, cook for another minute before turning off the heat. The dumplings should be slightly translucent. Drizzle a little oil over to prevent sticking, strain dumplings onto a large plate to serve.

15. To make the dipping sauce, mix all the ingredients together and portion into condiment dishes. Serve dumplings hot with the dipping sauce.

16. Cooked dumplings can be stored refrigerated in an airtight container for up to 5 days. They can also be frozen for 2 months. To cook frozen dumplings, use the same steps for boiling.

NOTES

- This recipe is probably the most complex one from this book. Don't fret if you can't get it right at first. If you are trying it for the first time, halve or quarter the recipe to practise.

- The amount of water for the dough actually depends on your brand of flour and room humidity. For brands of flour that have less moisture, use a bit more water. If you are in a dry climate, use about 100–200 ml more.

- If your dough is too sticky, add more flour. If you find it difficult to mix all the flour together, add a bit more water (50 ml at a time).

- For the filling, you can use other veggies and mushrooms, but avoid veggies that have high water content, like tomatoes. Pickled veggies like pickled radish (*chai poh*), kimchi or pickled Chinese mustard can be a nice addition, but do squeeze them slightly to remove excess water.

- Japanese scallion can be replaced with 4 Tbsp toon paste, or use 2–3 other ingredients listed above for a similar level of flavour complexity.

12a

- When wrapping, avoid puncturing the wrapper or getting any flour, oil or filling on the its edges at all costs. This prevents the dumpling from breaking when boiling. If you've made a hole accidentally, patch up by adding a tiny ball of dough over it and pinching it firmly.

- Keep your hands lightly floured while doing the wrapping, but avoid getting flour on the side with the filling. All surfaces that will touch uncooked dumplings should be floured too.

- When boiling, do not stir the pot with chopsticks or other sharp utensils as they may puncture the dumplings. As the filling is plant-based, we just need to ensure the wrapper gets cooked. Boiling the dumplings for too long may cause them to break.

- When storing, keep the dumplings flat and level to keep the shape.

- To make pan-fried dumplings from frozen dumplings, heat about 1 Tbsp oil in a frying pan. Place dumplings bottom down, cover the pan and fry over medium-low heat until browned.

12b

- If you have extra filling left, you can make veggie pancakes (page 107). If you have extra dough left, you can make traditional handmade noodles (page 31).

sides

char siu tempeh

Makes 20 bite-sized pieces

INGREDIENTS

200 g tempeh

2 blocks fermented red beancurd

1 Tbsp light soy sauce

1 Tbsp dark soy sauce

1 tsp five-spice powder

$1/4$ tsp ground white pepper

80–100 g sugar, or to taste

2 Tbsp sweet syrup like maltose or maple syrup

1 Tbsp sesame oil

80 ml ($1/3$ cup) mushroom stock, or as needed, from soaking or boiling dried shiitake mushrooms in water

1 tsp liquid smoke (optional but highly recommended)

METHOD

1. Use a fork to poke holes in tempeh. Cut tempeh into 10 x 5-cm blocks and steam for 8–10 minutes. Let cool and set aside.

2. Meanwhile, mix the remaining ingredients in a bowl to make the marinade. Transfer tempeh blocks to a shallow dish and spread them out in 1 layer. Pour the marinade in, making sure the tempeh is mostly covered. If not, top up with more stock and stir marinade carefully to mix. Cover dish with cling wrap and refrigerate overnight.

3. Preheat the oven to 200°C. Line a baking tray with aluminium foil and roll up the edges. Arrange tempeh in a row and pour over the remaining marinade. Bake for 40–50 minutes, or until more than half the marinade is reduced and tempeh is a dark brownish red. Flip tempeh and rotate baking tray midway for even heating.

4. Let rest until cool enough to handle. Slice and serve. Any remaining sauce can be kept together with the slices. These can be kept refrigerated in an airtight container for up to 5 days. To reheat, simply steam or toast for 2 minutes.

NOTES

- Steaming the tempeh gets rid of its pungent fermented beany smell, thus allowing the flavours of the marinade to shine.

- When marinating, ensure that all of the tempeh is covered for even marination. If your tempeh floats, simply place a clean small plate or utensil on top to press it down.

- Gluten-free options: swap the soy sauce for tamari or liquid aminos.

- Fermented red bean curd is a type of tofu cultured with red rice yeast. It can be replaced with other types of fermented bean curd, or with miso (preferably red miso).

- If you don't have five-spice powder, a mixture of ground nutmeg, cinnamon, black pepper and cloves is a decent substitute, although the flavour notes are slightly different.

- Sugar is needed to caramelise the sauce so that it's viscous enough to cling onto the tempeh. You can reduce its quantity but I don't recommend omitting it.

- Using maltose helps give the sauce its signature shiny appearance, so it's highly recommended. Other types of syrup sweeteners can work but to a lesser degree.

Char siu, which is Cantonese marinated and roasted pork slices, is a local favourite among the Chinese community. I chose tempeh for the "meat" mainly because it absorbs marinade well and has a firmer bite than tofu.

As with all fermented savoury foods, kimchi is a fantastic source of probiotics and packs an excellent umami. I love using them in soups, stir-fries, noodles, rice and savoury pancakes to add a bit of spice and tang. Traditional kimchi is made by fermenting cabbage with a cooked spicy rice paste. Here's a much simpler and quicker way for busy people, although not very traditional. This recipe is completely raw, as no cooking is needed!

easy kimchi

Makes about 1.5 kg kimchi

INGREDIENTS
KIMCHI

1 large napa cabbage (*wongbok* / Chinese cabbage), around 1–1.5kg

1/8 cup salt

1 cup hard, crisp veggie of your choice (carrot, celery, beetroot, red cabbage), finely chopped

PASTE

1 red bell pepper

3-cm knob ginger

1 stalk leek (onion, garlic or white part of spring onion can also be used)

2 Tbsp chilli powder or 4 bird's eye chillies (chilli padi), seeds removed, or to taste

2 Tbsp salt

METHOD

1. Wash and break or cut cabbage into bite-sized pieces. Place in a bowl, then rub and mix thoroughly with salt and leave aside.

2. For the paste, roughly chop bell pepper, ginger, leek and chillies. Place in a food processor or blender with salt and process into a paste. You can also use a mortar and pestle, or cut the veggies into tiny pieces before mixing with salt if you do not have the tools mentioned.

3. Sterilise a glass jar by pouring boiling water into it, then discard the water while wearing oven mittens for your safety.

4. By now the cabbage should have released some water. Combine the paste and crisp veggie of your choice with the cabbage. Wearing a pair of gloves, mix the vegetables using your hands until the paste is evenly distributed. Transfer to the prepared jar and press down firmly to keep veggies immersed in its liquid. If there is too little liquid, add a little water until the cabbage is submerged. Do not add too much, as it will over dilute the salt. Leave at least 5 cm of buffer space between the mixture and the jar opening as a lot of water will be released during fermentation.

5. Cover and leave the jar to sit at room temperature. To release built-up gas, unscrew and close the lid every day.

6. After 3 or 4 days (or longer if you are in a cold area), the kimchi should be ready to eat and should be stored in the refrigerator. If it still tastes slightly raw, let it ferment for longer. For an even deeper flavour, age for 1–2 days in the refrigerator. Any utensils used to handle kimchi should be clean and dry.

NOTES

- Allium-free options: omit leek and use more ginger and chilli.
- The chilli can be omitted if you prefer a non-spicy version.
- It's important to use only sterilised utensils to handle and store the ingredients and kimchi. Immerse all utensils and containers for at least 5 minutes in water that's just boiled.
- During fermentation, the cabbage may start floating. If that happens, push sterilised non-metal utensils into the mixture and cover the lid to keep the cabbage submerged at all times. I often use small cup covers or glass containers to do this. Anything that is not in contact with the salt water may start to spoil.
- Climate can greatly affect fermentation time. Kimchi ferments the fastest in a hot and humid place. If you are in a cold area and want a faster fermentation, wrap the jars in blankets.

monkey head mushroom satay

Makes 15–20 skewers

INGREDIENTS

SATAY

100–130 g dried monkey head mushrooms or 500 g frozen ones, soaked in warm water for at least 1 hour

100 g sugar

2 Tbsp cooking oil

20 bamboo or metal skewers (if using bamboo, soak them in water for 30 minutes)

MARINADE

300 g shallots, peeled and chopped

4 cloves garlic, peeled and chopped

3 stalks lemongrass, white part only, sliced

20 g ginger, peeled and chopped

15 g galangal, peeled and chopped

15 g turmeric, peeled and chopped

1 Tbsp ground cumin

1 tsp ground fennel

1 tsp ground coriander

1 tsp salt

METHOD

1. To prepare the mushrooms, discard the soaking water and squeeze the absorbed water from each mushroom. Discard this brown water and soak mushrooms again in clean water for 5 minutes. Repeat soaking and squeezing the mushrooms until the water that comes out from each one is clear. This removes the mushroom's bitter compounds.

2. Cut mushrooms into bite-sized pieces. If there are some parts that are too fibrous or difficult to cut, don't use these bits as they will be too tough to eat. You can reserve them for adding to clear soup (page 28) for extra nutrition.

3. In a blender, process all the marinade ingredients together until you get a paste.

4. Place mushrooms in a large bowl, add sugar and mix well. Add marinade, mix well and cover. Transfer to a large ziplock bag and seal it, removing as much air from the bag as possible. Using your hands, massage the mushrooms gently to ensure the marinade soaks into each piece. Let sit in the refrigerator for at least 3 hours.

5. Preheat the oven to 170ºC. Line a baking tray with aluminium foil and place a metal rack over it. This keeps your oven's bottom clean. Brush the rack generously with cooking oil.

PEANUT SAUCE

1 cup roasted unsalted peanuts

6–8 dried red chillies, or to taste, de-seeded, soaked in warm water and chopped

4 cloves garlic, peeled and chopped

4 shallots, peeled and chopped

2 stalks lemongrass, white parts only, chopped

1-inch knob galangal, peeled and chopped

1 tsp salt

60 ml (¼ cup) oil

250–500 ml (1–2 cups) water, as needed

1 Tbsp tamarind pulp, soaked in ¼ cup water for 15 minutes, squeezed to extract juice, pulp discarded

1 Tbsp sweet soy sauce (*kecap manis*)

2 Tbsp sugar, preferably palm sugar (*gula melaka*)

GARNISHES

2 red onions, peeled and cut into bite-sized pieces

1 cucumber, cut into bite-sized pieces

2–3 Malay rice cakes (*ketupat*), cut into bite-sized cubes

6. Thread 3–4 mushroom pieces onto each skewer. Baste mushrooms with cooking oil and arrange skewers on the rack. Bake for 15–20 minutes.

7. When mushrooms begin to brown, remove from the oven. Turn skewers over, baste with the remaining marinade and more cooking oil. Bake for another 15–20 minutes, until the mushrooms are browned and some edges slightly charred.

8. In the meantime, prepare the peanut sauce. Crush peanuts coarsely with a mortar and pestle or food processor and set aside. In a clean food processor or blender, blend chillies, garlic, shallots, lemongrass, galangal and salt until you get a fine paste. If mixture is difficult to blend, add 1 or 2 Tbsp water to help it along.

9. Heat oil over low heat and fry spice paste for 6–8 minutes until aromatic and a reddish oil seeps out. Add peanuts and water, then cook for 2–3 minutes. Add tamarind juice, sweet soy sauce and sugar, then mix well. Keep the heat low and let the sauce simmer while stirring continuously for 2–3 minutes until smooth. Add more water if needed. Taste and season with more tamarind, sugar or soy sauce if preferred. Transfer to a sauce bowl and let cool. You should see a layer of red oil on top of the sauce.

10. To serve, arrange satay on a large plate. Place sauce and garnishes of your choice on the side.

NOTES

- This can be cooked over a grill or barbecue too. It's almost impossible to fully replicate the charred smokiness in a home kitchen, but adding a 1 tsp liquid smoke will add a nice smokiness.

- I recommend using dried monkey head mushrooms as frozen ones are often harder. But if you're using frozen ones, you don't have to soak and squeeze them.

- Soaking bamboo skewers in warm water for 30 minutes before threading the mushrooms prevents the skewers from burning.

- Allium-free option: omit garlic and shallots, then double the amount of lemongrass and ginger called for.

- If you don't have ground cumin, fennel and coriander, you can use a tablespoon of any spice mix. The taste will be slightly different but it works as a decent substitute.

- To remove pungency from the onions for garnishing, soak them in water for 10 minutes and drain before serving.

- Some brands of peanuts are drier, so add more water for the peanut paste if you need to. Taste after adding water and adjust the seasoning with more sweet soy sauce, salt or tamarind if preferred.

- The satay sauce can be made up to 2 days in advance. In fact, the flavour develops further when the sauce is refrigerated. You can also make the marinade a day in advance and marinate the satay overnight for best flavour.

- Excess peanut sauce can be mopped up with bread or even used to top noodles!

- Excess marinade can be used to marinate tofu, tempeh or other proteins you like.

Serving suggestion

Satay is undoubtedly a favourite street food in Southeast Asia. Different countries in the region have their own versions of skewered meat grilled over an open charcoal grill and served with a rich and savoury dipping sauce. This is inspired by the Malaysian version, which is paired with a sweet and savoury peanut sauce, and often served with *ketupat* (rice cakes), red onions and cucumbers. Monkey head mushroom, also called lion's mane mushroom, is a fantastic meat alternative in this case because it can be cooked to a tender and juicy texture while absorbing flavours perfectly. It's also known as a superfood in Chinese medicine. It comes either frozen (usually processed with soy protein) or dried (fully natural). Dried unprocessed monkey head mushrooms are a bit tricky to prepare due to a natural bitter compound. It takes a few extra steps to remove it, but I think it's worth it considering the mushroom's health benefits and wonderful texture.

Fish is used in many Asian dishes like fish *bee hoon* soup (Chinese rice noodles with fish) and *assam pedas* (tangy and spicy Malay fish curry). My aim is not to copy the taste of animal protein exactly, but to give a new take on flavours that are familiar. Here I used tempeh as the base protein, as it can absorb flavours excellently and cook to a very tender texture. The main difference between plant and animal proteins is that plant proteins are mild on their own. Extra effort is needed to impart and coax flavours out of them. Thus there are a few extra steps to impart a briny "ocean" flavour and moist texture.

seaweed tempeh slices

Makes 6 slices, about 600g

INGREDIENTS

1 Tbsp fermented bean paste

1 Tbsp salted black beans

1 Tbsp soy sauce

1 tsp ground white pepper

10 x 5-cm piece dried kelp (kombu), cleaned according to packet instructions, or 2 Tbsp dried wakame

200 g tempeh, cut into 11 x 5 x 0.5-cm pieces

250 ml (1 cup) stock, or as needed

3 sheets ready-to-eat sushi seaweed (nori), about 20 x 18 cm each, or as needed

2 Tbsp white cornflour

Juice from 1 lime

2–3 Tbsp cooking oil, or as needed

METHOD

1. In a bowl, crush fermented bean paste using a spoon. Add black beans, soy sauce and pepper and mix well. Place kelp in a separate large bowl and cover with stock and bean paste mixture.

2. Add tempeh to the marinade and make sure the kelp is in contact with the tempeh and stock. Cover with foil and marinate in the refrigerator overnight.

3. Cut each seaweed sheet in half.

4. Remove tempeh from the marinade. Reserve all the marinade and mix 3 Tbsp with cornflour until you get a sticky paste. Dip tempeh into this paste then wrap with a piece of seaweed. Dip the end of the seaweed sheet in marinade to secure it to the tempeh. Repeat to use up tempeh and seaweed.

5. Heat oil in a pan over medium-low heat and add the wrapped tempeh along with 5–6 Tbsp marinade. Fry until tempeh is browned. Drain and set aside on paper towels. Repeat until all slices are fried.

6. Cut into bite-sized pieces before serving if preferred. The slices can be refrigerated for up to 5 days, or kept frozen for 2 months.

NOTES

•   If you want to reduce the amount of oil used, bake the tempeh instead or fry with less oil in a non-stick pan.

•   If you don't like the beany flavour of tempeh, boil or steam it shortly before adding to the marinade to reduce the taste.

•   These can be made in bulk when you have time and kept frozen for a convenient and tasty protein food.

•   Cornflour helps in binding and giving a crispy texture when the tempeh is freshly fried. Others like tapioca or potato flour will work, but they may not give the same texture.

•   Gluten-free options: swap the soy sauce for tamari or liquid aminos.

•   The leftover kelp can be used in soups or stir-fries. The marinade can be reused to flavour tempeh, tofu or seitan.

4d

4e

soy sauce chickpeas and nuts

Serves 4

INGREDIENTS

SPICES & SEASONING

3 star anise

1 stick cinnamon

8–10 white peppercorns

8–10 black peppercorns

1–2 bird's eye chilli (chilli padi), halved lengthwise, seeds removed (omit if you prefer this dish non-spicy)

1-cm knob ginger, peeled and sliced

5 x 5-cm piece dried kelp (kombu), cleaned according to packet instructions, or 2 Tbsp dried wakame

A pinch of asafoetida (optional, omit if you don't take alliums)

3 Tbsp premium soy sauce

1 Tbsp sugar, to taste

BEANS & NUTS

1 1/2 cups dried chickpeas

2 litres (8 cups) water, or as needed

1/2 cup raw cashews (other nuts like peanuts, walnuts or Chinese almonds can be used too)

METHOD

1. Soak chickpeas or beans of choice in water for 12 hours. Discard the soaking water and give the beans a rinse.

2. Place beans, nuts, spices and seasoning in a pot. Add 2 litres (8 cups) water or enough to cover ingredients fully. Bring to a boil over medium heat, then remove the kelp.

3. Cook over medium-low heat for 1.5–2 hours. If it becomes too dry before the beans are cooked, add another 125 ml (1/2 cup) water to prevent burning. Cook until water is almost absorbed. Transfer into a bowl and serve hot, or leave to cool before storing.

NOTES

*   Any type of bean can be used, as long as the bean won't split too much or disintegrate after cooking for a long time — for this reason, avoid split lentils and mung beans.

*   Soak beans overnight for best results and digestibility.

*   To prevent drying out the pot and burning the beans, check every 30–40 minutes. Add more water if needed.

*   This can be made in a rice or slow cooker too. Choose a suitable setting for beans.

*   Gluten-free options: swap the soy sauce for tamari or liquid aminos.

This oil-free, one-pot and protein-rich recipe is a staple in my food prep repertoire. It's easy to make and keeps well in the fridge. This was inspired by my mother's signature slow-cooked tofu. Firm tofu pieces are slowly stewed and left to sit overnight in a lip-smacking, umami-rich broth. This slow-cooking method is know as *lu* (卤) in Chinese cuisine. It relies on low, constant heat; total immersion of ingredients; and a mix of good sauces and spices. The secret to maximum flavour in this recipe is reducing the amount of liquid to as little as possible (without burning) so taste is concentrated in the beans and nuts itself. Thus, controlling the water amount is most important.

This is the plant-based version of a staple Chinese home dish that many grew up with. Juicy tomatoes mingle with softly scrambled tofu in a saucy dish that goes perfectly with rice. Tomatoes are packed with umami and savouriness. The uneven tofu pieces catch the sauce while adding protein. Although tofu doesn't behave exactly like eggs under heat, this recipe is still nutritious and familiar.

tomato tofu scramble

Serves 2

INGREDIENTS

150 ml aquafaba (roughly liquid from 1 can of chickpeas)

300 g soft tofu

$1/4$ tsp + $1/2$ tsp black salt

A pinch of ground turmeric (optional, for colour)

1 Tbsp oil

3 medium ripe tomatoes, diced

$1/2$ Tbsp light soy sauce

METHOD

1. In a pot, bring aquafaba to a gentle boil over medium-low heat and let simmer until it is reduced by half. Remove from heat and leave to cool.

2. Gently press the soft tofu to remove excess water.

3. Blend cooled aquafaba, tofu, $1/4$ tsp black salt and turmeric in a blender or food processor until you get a smooth, pale yellow creamy mixture.

4. In a flat non-stick pan, heat oil over medium heat. When oil is hot, add tofu mixture and reduce heat to medium-low. Let the liquid reduce and simmer until tofu mixture is lightly browned on the underside. This will take about 15–20 minutes or more, depending on the size of your pan. Do not stir or scramble, but check at 8-minute intervals for any sticking by using a wooden or silicone spatula to gently push the sides and bottom.

5. When the underside is lightly browned, add tomatoes and soy sauce. Let everything simmer over medium heat for 10 minutes or so to reduce the liquid, until the sides of the tofu mixture can be picked up gently without breaking too much, and the tomatoes "melt" to take on an almost sauce-like consistency. Gently press down on the tomato pieces to release more liquid to mix with the tofu, but do not stir or scramble the mixture.

6. Turn off the heat and sprinkle with $1/2$ tsp black salt before transferring everything to a plate. The tofu will break slightly and that's perfectly fine as we want uneven pieces for textural variation. Taste and season with more black salt if preferred. Serve hot with rice.

NOTES

*   Because this recipe is pretty simple, using good quality tomatoes is important.
*   Cook this only in a flat non-stick pan as reducing moisture gradually is most important in this recipe. If not, you may just get a watery yellow tofu puree!
*   If you want chunks of the tofu to remain, do not stir or scramble. Tofu doesn't behave like egg, as its proteins do not coagulate as fast as egg proteins do. If you scramble or stir the mixture, you will get a yellow and red mixture that's almost similar to baby food.
*   Black salt is the main seasoning here, which gives this dish an egg-like umami taste. If you don't have it, you can use more soy sauce instead.

tempeh rendang

Serves 2

INGREDIENTS

1/3 cup shredded coconut

2 Tbsp oil

6 kaffir lime leaves, scrunched up to release fragrance

1 stick cinnamon

2–3 cloves

1 star anise

2–3 cardamom pods

3 stalks lemongrass, green parts only, bruised to release fragrance

200 g tempeh, cut into bite-sized cubes

1 Tbsp tamarind pulp, soaked in 1/4 cup warm water and strained to discard seeds

2 tsp salt, or to taste

1 tsp sugar, or to taste

250 ml (1 cup) coconut milk

500 ml (2 cups) water

Juice from 1 lime

REMPAH

5 cloves garlic, peeled and crushed

5 shallots, crushed and peeled

2.5-cm knob galangal, peeled and chopped

2.5-cm knob ginger, peeled and chopped

3 stalks lemongrass, white part only, very finely chopped

3–10 dried red chillies, soaked and deseeded (more or less, to taste)

GARNISHES

1 sprig coriander

Kaffir lime leaves, finely cut

METHOD

1. Place shredded coconut in a dry pan over low heat and stir until golden brown. Set aside.

2. Pound all the *rempah* ingredients in a mortar and pestle, or process in a food processor into a paste.

3. Heat oil in a wok over medium-high heat and fry *rempah* until fragrant. Add kaffir lime leaves, cinnamon, cloves, star anise, cardamom and lemongrass, then fry until fragrant.

4. Add tempeh and stir to mix with spices and paste. Add tamarind water, toasted coconut, salt, sugar, coconut milk and water. Cover and simmer over low heat until liquid is almost reduced, which may take 1–3 hours.

5. Taste and season with lime juice and more salt if preferred. Garnish as preferred and serve hot with rice. Leftovers can be kept refrigerated for up to 3 days.

NOTES

- If you wish to save time, make the spice paste in bulk. Mine kept well refrigerated for 1 week.

- The flavours and aromas for this dish are stronger the next day. Make a big portion so you can have it again!

- It may be tricky to replicate the exact same flavour without alliums. Allium-free option: use 1 1/2 Tbsp toon paste with 1 tsp ground turmeric in place of garlic and shallots, while increasing the amount of other aromatics like shredded coconut, ginger, galangal, kaffir lime leaves and lemongrass.

2

Rendang is a rich, spicy and tender stew that's incredibly popular in Malaysia, Indonesia and Singapore. Here tempeh is used to make an explosively flavourful and high-protein accompaniment for rice or breads. Thanks to the bold spices and rich coconut milk used, plain blocks of tempeh can be transformed into a wonderful dish.

light bites

chinese spring rolls

Makes 15–18 rolls

INGREDIENTS

4 water chestnuts, peeled

5 dried shiitake mushrooms, soaked

20 g dried bean noodles (*tung hoon*), soaked

320 g firm tofu, about 3 blocks, cut into small cubes

2 Tbsp + 60 ml (¼ cup) cooking oil

2-cm knob ginger, peeled and minced

2 tsp sesame oil

2 Tbsp light soy sauce

1 tsp dark soy sauce

30 g chives, about 5 stalks, finely chopped

1 tsp ground white pepper

1 tsp sea salt, to taste

1 tsp cornstarch

3 Tbsp water

15–18 sheets square spring roll pastry skins, or as needed

METHOD

1. Chop water chestnuts roughly and squeeze with your hands to remove excess water. Place in a food processor with drained shiitake and bean noodles, then blend together. Set aside.

2. Place tofu in a cheesecloth bag. Squeeze excess water out gently but firmly — you don't want to mash it too much.

3. Transfer to a pan or wok, then add 2 Tbsp cooking oil. Stir-fry for 1–2 minutes until light brown. Remove from heat, stir in ginger, sesame oil and soy sauces. Transfer to a large bowl and add the blended mixture and chives.

4. Taste it at this point and season with pepper, salt or more soy sauce. It should taste much saltier than what you prefer. In a small bowl mix cornstarch and water.

5. To wrap, place about 2 Tbsp filling into every square pastry skin. Of course, this amount will vary depending on the size and shape of your pastry skin. Roll up one end to cover the filling, fold both sides in and roll up to the other end. Dab the cornstarch mixture at the sides and press gently to seal.

6. Heat the remaining cooking oil in a pan and pan-fry the spring rolls over medium-low heat, flipping to ensure even cooking. You can also deep-fry them in a pot of oil or bake for 20–30 minutes at 220°C. Before baking, brush each roll generously with oil for best results.

7. When spring rolls are mostly golden brown, drain them of excess oil on paper towels before serving. Store any leftovers in the refrigerator or freezer. These are best reheated in a toaster oven for a crunchy shell.

NOTES

*   The filling should be moist but not wet. If it's too wet, add more dried bean noodles to help absorb excess water.

*   Gluten-free option: use 2–3 sheets rice paper wrappers for each spring roll. Use liquid aminos or tamari instead of soy sauce.

*   Allium-free option: chives can be replaced with other veggies or mushrooms like carrots, zucchini, Chinese gourd, radish, bok choy, straw mushrooms and more. Avoid veggies that have high water content, like tomatoes. Pickled veggies like pickled radish (*chai poh*), kimchi, or pickled Chinese mustard can be a nice addition, but do squeeze them lightly to remove excess water.

*   For veggies with high water content, such as cabbage, radish, celery and so on, blitz in a food processor first, then squeeze out excess water through a cheesecloth before mixing with other ingredients. For ingredients with strong flavours like chives and shiitake, don't squeeze them so that they will retain their full flavours.

Spring rolls are quite labour intensive, but they can be made ahead and kept frozen for months. An excellent "emergency" food, or for when you're craving for a crispy, savoury snack. They can be easily reheated in a microwave, oven or toaster oven. The ready-made spring roll skin can be purchased from the frozen section of supermarkets or Asian stores.

dal and quinoa masala patties

Makes 16–18 patties

INGREDIENTS
PATTIES

1 cup yellow lentils

$1/4$ cup uncooked quinoa, rinsed well

A pinch of asafoetida (optional)

$1^1/2$ Tbsp cooking oil + more for brushing

1 Tbsp mustard seeds

1 cardamom pod

1 clove

3 cloves garlic, peeled and roughly chopped

1-cm knob ginger, peeled and sliced

$1/4$ cup cashews, chopped

5 Tbsp garam masala

1 Chinese mountain yam, about 8 cm in length, peeled

1 cup rolled oats

$2^1/2$ tsp salt

A small bunch of coriander, chopped

Juice from half a lemon or lime

GREEN CHUTNEY

1 cup mint leaves

$1/2$ cup chopped coriander leaves

1–2 cloves garlic, peeled (or 1 Tbsp toon paste)

1 tsp lemon juice, or to taste

A pinch of red chilli powder, or to taste

1. To make the chutney, blend all the ingredients together.

2. Soak lentils and quinoa together for at least an hour. Discard the soaking water and rinse before cooking.

3. Place the lentils and quinoa in a large pot. Add asafoetida and enough water to cover. Bring to a boil and simmer over medium-low heat for 15–20 minutes. When quinoa shows tails and lentils are easily mashed, drain, set aside and let cool.

4. Heat a frying pan over medium-low heat and add oil. When oil is hot, add mustard seeds and fry until they start popping. Add cardamom, clove, garlic, ginger and cashews. Lightly stir to ensure even heating. When cashews are lightly browned, turn off the heat. Pick out and discard the cardamom and clove. Add garam masala to the pan and mix well with the sautéed cashews, garlic and ginger. Let cool for 10 minutes.

5. Grate Chinese mountain yam over a bowl to obtain a white liquid with the consistency of egg whites.

6. In a large mixing bowl, place oats, cashew mixture, lentils and quinoa, mountain yam, lemon juice, coriander and salt. Mix well while mashing the mixture using a spatula or large fork. The mixture should start becoming sticky and will be able to hold together easily. If the mixture is still warm at this point, place in the refrigerator to cool for 15 minutes.

7. Preheat the oven to 180°C. Line a baking tray with baking paper. Shape the mixture into balls around 5 cm in diameter and place on the prepared baking tray. Flatten each ball slightly and brush the patties' tops and sides with oil.

8. Bake for 25 minutes, rotating tray halfway through baking. You can also shallow-fry or deep-fry these for crispier patties. Serve warm with green chutney or let cool completely on a wire rack before storing in airtight containers. These can be kept in the refrigerator for 5 days and in the freezer for 2 months.

NOTES

- If you don't have garam masala, use other powdered spice mixes. If you don't have whole spices, use more garlic, ginger and an extra 1 Tbsp garam masala; or add around $1/4$ cup curry powder and more garam masala.

- If you don't have Chinese yam, add $1/2$ cup mashed potatoes, or 2 Tbsp flaxseed powder. Oats also have a binding effect as they absorb liquid.

- Allium-free options: garlic can be omitted and more asafoetida, mustard seeds, ginger added to achieve a similar strength of aroma.

- Gluten-free option: use gluten-free oats.

This is inspired by a traditional savoury snack popular across India called *tikki*. This adapted, non-traditional recipe is basically a protein-packed patty made with spices, lentils and quinoa. You can eat it as it is or use it as a burger patty, to fill a sandwich or to top off a salad. I made this lunch box item easy to pack, satisfying, reheatable and freezer-friendly. It's packed with complex carbs, complete proteins and good fats. Because of the wonderful natural binding secret ingredient used, you can literally throw anything into the mixture and it still binds perfectly! You can add veggies like finely chopped broccoli, peas, carrots and beetroot, and grains like rice or barley — a fantastic way to clear out the fridge! This pairs great with a refreshing and tangy green chutney, a condiment that's often served with various kinds of Indian snacks.

Another delicious addition to lunch boxes, these can be served at parties as finger food or even placed in your sandwiches or burgers. Usually Japanese croquettes are deep-fried, and you can't find a vegan version easily. For this recipe, since the ingredients for the croquettes are already cooked, you only need less than 2.5 cm oil to shallow-fry the outside. I've added wakame, shiitake and carrots for extra flavour, colour and nutrition. To bind the ingredients together so that the mixture can be shaped and fried without breaking, eggs are most commonly use. Here, I used grated mountain yam (*nagaimo* or *yamaimo*) instead, which can be easily replaced with flaxseed (see notes).

japanese-style potato and lentil croquettes

Makes 20–22 pieces

INGREDIENTS

CROQUETTES

1 litre (4 cups) water

250 g red lentils, soaked for at least 30 minutes

3 potatoes, peeled and diced

Neutral-flavored oil (vegetable, canola, etc.) as needed

1 onion, peeled and finely diced

1 tsp salt

$1/2$ carrot, finely diced

2 shiitake mushrooms, finely diced

2 Tbsp dried wakame, soaked, drained and finely chopped

1 Tbsp light soy sauce

$1/4$ tsp ground white pepper

Freshly ground black pepper

7.5-cm length Chinese mountain yam, peeled

BREADING

1 cup all-purpose flour

250 ml (1 cup) non-dairy milk

2 cups panko (Japanese breadcrumbs)

METHOD

1. In a large pot, place water, lentils and potatoes and bring to a boil. Cook over medium heat until lentils are easily mashed and a fork goes through the potatoes easily. This might take about 20 minutes. Drain through a fine mesh sieve before returning potatoes and lentils to the pot. Over low heat, let everything cook for a few minutes, stirring to prevent burning, until remaining moisture is completely evaporated. Turn off the heat and mash everything, mixing until combined. Set aside.

2. In a pan, heat 1 Tbsp oil over medium heat. Sauté onions with salt until soft and translucent. Add carrots, shiitake, wakame, soy sauce and ground peppers, and cook until soft. Set aside.

3. Grate Chinese mountain yam over a bowl to obtain a white liquid with the consistency of egg whites. In a large mixing bowl add mashed mixture, grated yam and cooked vegetables. Mix well until combined, then set aside to cool until manageable with your hands. You should get a mixture that can be pressed together with your hands. Shape a small handful of it into a ball and press slightly to flatten it. Repeat to use up the mixture.

4. Dip each patty in flour, followed by non-dairy milk, then coat generously with panko.

5. In a wok or frying pan, heat 250 ml (1 cup) oil over medium-high heat. Shallow-fry patties until golden brown, then transfer onto paper towels to drain. Cook in batches of 3–5 patties so as not to overcrowd the pan. Top up with more oil if needed. Serve hot with your preferred sauce. You can store leftovers refrigerated in an airtight container for up to 7 days. They can also be frozen for up to a month. Simply reheat by baking in an oven or toaster oven at 180ºC for 10–15 minutes.

NOTES

*   Feel free to replace the red lentils with other types of lentils or beans, as long as they can be cooked until soft and mashed to mix with the potato.

*   If you don't have mountain yam, replace it with 1 flax "egg". Stir 1 Tbsp flaxseed powder with 3 Tbsp water and let sit for 10 minutes until you get a gooey brown mixture.

*   You can replace wakame, shiitake and carrots with other ingredients as long as they can be finely chopped.

*   Gluten-free options: replace all-purpose flour with almond meal or gluten-free oatmeal. You can also use gluten-free panko or process dry gluten-free bread to make your own crumbs for coating.

*   Allium-free options: replace onion with 1 Tbsp toon paste, or use finely chopped celery and increase the amount of spices for more fragrance.

lentil tofu murtabak

Makes 10 pieces

Oil as needed

2 stalks spring onions, green part only, chopped finely

DOUGH

4 cups bread flour

40 g oil + more for coating

1 Tbsp coconut milk (or other non-dairy milks)

310 ml (1^1/$_4$ cups) water

FILLING

350 g firm tofu

^{1}/$_2$ tsp + ^{1}/$_2$ tsp ground black pepper

^{1}/$_2$ tsp + ^{1}/$_2$ tsp ground turmeric

1^1/$_2$ Tbsp soy sauce

1 Tbsp + 1^1/$_2$ Tbsp oil

^{1}/$_2$ large onion, peeled and diced

2 heaping Tbsp spice mix powder (garam masala works best)

600–800 ml water, or as needed

2 tsp salt

250 g red lentils, soaked for at least 1 hour

1. Prepare the dough the day before. Place all the ingredients in a large mixing bowl and mix together to form a dough. Knead with oiled hands for 10 minutes, then cover the bowl with a moist paper towel to prevent dough from drying out. Leave to rest at room temperature for 30 minutes, then knead again for another 5 minutes.

2. Form dough into a log and cut into 10 equal pieces. Roll each piece into a palm-sized ball and coat generously with cooking oil. Place in a greased container to prevent sticking. Cover tightly with cling film or a lid and refrigerate overnight.

3. To make the filling, start by removing excess water from the tofu. I do this by gently squeezing the tofu, then letting it sit for 15 minutes on a sieve placed over a bowl. In another bowl, use a fork to mash the drained tofu with ^{1}/$_2$ tsp pepper, ^{1}/$_2$ tsp turmeric and soy sauce. In a non-stick frying pan, heat 1 Tbsp oil over medium heat and scramble the tofu mixture. Stop when mixture is yellow and most of the excess moisture is evaporated. Taste to check that it's saltier than what you prefer. Season with more soy sauce if you like. Remove from heat and set aside.

4. In a pot, heat 1^1/$_2$ Tbsp oil over medium heat. Add onion and sauté until translucent. Add spice mix powder and the remaining pepper and turmeric, stirring in a quick motion to coat the onion. Add water and salt, then bring to a boil. Reduce heat to medium-low, add lentils and ensure the water just covers them. Cook for 20–30 minutes, stirring gently to prevent sticking to the bottom. Stop when the water is absorbed and lentils become soft but not mashed together. Taste to check that it's saltier than what you prefer. Season with more salt if you like. Set aside to cool.

A murtabak is a flatbread with Arabic origins that's stuffed with a savoury spiced filling and fried until golden brown and crisp. In Singapore and Malaysia, it's a popular street food and some restaurants specialise in it. Finding a vegan version is rare, as it usually contains meat, butter and eggs, so I've developed my own recipe. This can be a bit tricky to make but trust me, if you get it right, it may be the most delicious thing you'll ever make! This can be made in advance and reheated, so it's a high-protein and filling option for adding to lunch boxes.

5. To assemble, coat a large, clean and smooth surface generously with oil. Keep $1/2$ cup oil handy. Flatten a dough ball with your palm. Press against the centre of the dough in an outward motion to push and stretch it as thin possible, until almost translucent and you can see the countertop through the dough without it tearing. If the dough starts to stick to your hands as you stretch it, coat your palms with oil. You can also lift one edge of the dough carefully and pull it gently outwards to stretch it even more.

6. Place 3–4 Tbsp lentil mixture in the centre of the dough. Flatten slightly and use your hand to shape it into a rectangle. Top with 1 heaping Tbsp scrambled tofu and sprinkle some chopped spring onions over. Fold the dough over the filling. It will overlap in the middle, so this will be the thicker side. Ensure the filling is fully covered.

7. To cook, heat about 1 Tbsp oil in a non-stick pan over low heat. Place a murtabak onto the pan with its thicker side down and cook over for 8–10 minutes until golden brown and crispy on one side. Check by carefully lifting up from one edge using a spatula. Flip to cook on the other side, topping up the pan with more oil if needed. Since the other side is thinner, it will cook more quickly. Once it's golden brown and crispy, transfer to a cooling rack. Repeat to assemble and cook the remaining murtabak one by one.

8. Serve hot with your favourite curry. To store, let cool completely and refrigerate for up to 7 days in an airtight container. To freeze, wrap each piece in cling film or freezer-friendly baking paper and place in an airtight container. To reheat, simple pan-fry on both sides with a bit of oil over medium-low heat.

NOTES

- To turn this into a balanced meal, you can add veggies like chopped beets, carrots, peas or mushrooms to the filling.

- Other types of beans or lentils like split chickpeas, split pigeon peas, small yellow lentils or green lentils can be used too. Avoid using whole beans as it will make the filling too chunky, and you will lose the murtabak's soft and even mouthfeel.

- It's important to avoid cooking the lentils to a dal-like consistency, or else the dough gets soggy and difficult to handle. The lentils should be soft enough to mash with your fingers, yet retain most of their shape.

- Allium-free options: you can use asafoetida, chopped tomatoes, minced mushrooms, toon paste, minced ginger, chopped celery, coriander or parsley stems to replace onions in this recipe. Feel free to use more than one type to find your favourite combination.

- You can use other types of flour like all-purpose flour, though bread flour is recommended as it has the highest gluten content, which helps the dough stretch as thinly as possible without breaking.

- If the dough breaks during stretching, don't worry. Simply scrunch the dough up into a ball, knead to combine and start over again.

- If the dough breaks while being folded over the filling, pull a piece of dough from a thicker part to fix the hole.

- If you find handling thin dough difficult, don't worry! Just make it as thin as you can manage and increase the cooking time on each side to ensure the dough is properly cooked.

- If your dough ends up too thick and not fully cooked, you can fry it with the frying pan slightly covered. This helps retain some moisture that will cook the insides. Do not cover the pan fully as the dough will retain too much moisture, and the murtabak will not end up as crisp. Thus, it's ideal to cut your first piece open after frying to check if the dough is fully cooked.

- I highly recommend frying each piece immediately after assembling. The dough is very soft, so if left to sit on the counter it will sink into the filling and start to tear.

This is a fun way to eat quinoa and is also perfect for anyone wanting to eat a low-carb high-protein dish or avoid refined grains. Quinoa is high in complete proteins. Although it is not as sticky as sushi rice, you can achieve a decently sticky texture. The trick is to only use white quinoa and let it sit in the pot for a while after cooking. Feel free to use regular sushi rice if you like. *Konnyaku* is a starchy root from traditional Japanese cuisine. It's high in fibre while being a low calorie food. *Konnyaku* is springy and chewy — similar to certain types of seafood. There's a lot of textures going on here with soft quinoa, springy *konnyaku* and creamy avocado!

quinoa avocado konnyaku sushi

Makes 20–22 pieces

INGREDIENTS

1 cup uncooked white quinoa, rinsed

310 ml (2¼ cups) water, or as needed

125 ml (½ cup) rice vinegar

2 Tbsp sugar

1 tsp salt

1 Tbsp miso, or as needed

3 sheets nori, or as needed

FILLING

½ block *konnyaku*, about 125 g, or as needed, cut into long thin pieces

1 avocado, peeled and sliced

½ carrot, julienned

CONDIMENTS

2 Tbsp sushi soy sauce, or light soy sauce

Wasabi, to taste

Red ginger pickles

METHOD

1. Blanch *konnyaku* in boiling water for 10 seconds to remove its smell. Drain and set aside to cool.

2. Add quinoa and water to a medium saucepan over high heat. The quinoa should be just covered by the water. Bring to a boil, then lower the heat and cover. Cook until translucent and the quinoa's tails are visible. Turn off the heat and let sit, covered, for 15 minutes. This will help get the quinoa to a stickier texture.

3. In the meantime, in a small saucepan over medium heat, add vinegar, sugar and salt. Stir until sugar and salt are dissolved. Pour vinegar mixture over warm quinoa, mix well, cover and let sit for 5–10 minutes until vinegar mixture is fully absorbed. Uncover and let cool completely.

4. Score *konnyaku* pieces, then spread a thin layer of miso over.

5. To assemble, place a bamboo mat on a flat surface and lay one sheet of nori on top. Wet your hands to prevent quinoa from sticking, then spread a layer of quinoa on the nori, leaving a slight border along the edges. Press the quinoa down to make it stick.

6. Place *konnyaku* slices near the edge of the quinoa, followed by avocado slices and julienned carrot.

7. To roll, start with the end closest to you. Using a bamboo mat, bring the end up and tightly roll over the filling, pressing as you go. Press the edges of the seaweed together to seal. If the edges aren't sealing, moisten them with a little water and press them together again.

8. With a sharp knife, cut the roll into 6–8 slices. Serve with condiments as preferred. The leftovers can be kept refrigerated in an airtight container for up to 2 days.

NOTES

*   Letting cooked quinoa sit covered in the pot for at least 15 minutes helps it develop a sticky texture, so the grains will not fall apart.

*   If you don't have *konnyaku*, replace it with any vegetable or mushroom you prefer. Carrots, cooked shiitake, seasoned tofu, cucumber, pickled Japanese radish work well here.

*   If you have extra *konnyaku*, you can make sweet and savoury skewers called miso *dengaku*. Cut *konnyaku* into strips and boil them lightly. Score the top with a knife, then skewer them. Boil 3 Tbsp miso, 3 Tbsp sugar, 2 Tbsp mirin (or 1 Tbsp mild-tasting vinegar) and 1 Tbsp cooking alcohol (optional but highly recommended) over low heat. Stir until sugar is dissolved and a glossy paste forms. Simply spread the paste on the *konnyaku* pieces and serve.

tempeh bak kwa

Makes 12–15 bite-sized pieces

INGREDIENTS

FOR BASE

400 g tempeh

125 ml (½ cup) neutral-tasting oil

MARINADE

1 Tbsp red rice yeast or a few drops of red colouring (optional, for colour)

2 blocks fermented red beancurd

2 Tbsp ground flaxseed powder

125 ml (½ cup) stock

90 g sugar

1 Tbsp light soy sauce

1 Tbsp dark soy sauce

½ Tbsp rice wine (optional)

1 Tbsp maltose (or any mild-tasting, light-coloured syrup)

2 Tbsp sesame oil

½ tsp five-spice powder, or to taste

½ tsp ground ginger, or to taste

½ tsp chilli powder, or to taste

½ tsp ground white pepper powder, or to taste

½ tsp ground black pepper, or to taste

1 tsp liquid smoke (optional but highly recommended)

½ Tbsp white miso or fermented bean paste

1 tsp marmite (optional)

GLAZE

1 Tbsp maltose

1 Tbsp water or red water (see method)

METHOD

1. Steam tempeh for 5–10 minutes and let cool before placing in a food processor and blending with oil into a thick, smooth paste.

2. Make red water for marinade. Mix ½ cup hot water and red rice yeast in a bowl, or combine in a pot and bring to a boil. Strain and let cool. Set aside 1 Tbsp red water for the glaze.

3. Add remaining red water and marinade ingredients to the blended tempeh in the food processor. Blend until combined and well mixed.

4. Transfer tempeh paste to a bowl. Cover and refrigerate overnight or for at least 6 hours.

5. Preheat the oven to 180°C. Line a baking tray with baking paper. Using a spatula, spread a layer of chilled paste, about 0.4-cm thick, on the prepared tray. The edges will be thinner, so gently push them inwards a little to minimise any burning. Spread cling film over the paste and flatten with a rolling pin.

6. Bake for about 25 minutes until paste is dry to the touch and able to be lifted slightly in one piece. Set aside to cool slightly.

7. Meanwhile, increase the oven temperature to 230°C. Mix the ingredients for the glaze together.

8. Cut baked paste into bite-sized slices. Brush one side of each slice with glaze and arrange glaze-side up on a lined baking tray.

9. Bake for 7–10 minutes then flip each slice over and glaze the other side. Grill in the oven for another 5 minutes or until slightly charred. Watch carefully here, as at this point the tempeh burns easily!

10. Remove from the oven and let cool. Minimise touching the slices when hot, as they break easily but will harden when cooled. Brush cooled slices with the remaining glaze to make them look shinier, if preferred. These can be kept refrigerated in an airtight container for 1–2 weeks.

NOTES

- Unlike meat, tempeh has very low fat and water content. Steaming gets rid of its fermented beany taste and introduces moisture, while adding oil "fattens"it. This is important for achieving a moist and rich texture.

- Flaxseed powder is vital as its proteins bind everything so that your *bak kwa* won't become bacon crumbles upon being touched!

- Don't spread the paste thinner than 0.3–0.4 cm as it will burn quite easily. Timing control is really important – remove immediately if you start to see smoke. If it's black and bitter, it's too burnt to eat.

- To prevent sticking, store each slice between greased or baking paper.

- Gluten-free options: swap soy sauce for tamari or amino seasoning.

Bak kwa is a well-loved local Chinese New Year snack that originated from Fujian in South China, made by smoking and preserving pork. Our traditional festival foods are very rich as they are meant to be eaten only once a year. I've created a tempeh version as a cholesterol-free, plant-based alternative. When done right, there's a sweet crispness on the surface with moist, smoky, savoury and chewy insides.

I have fond memories of my mother feeding me tomato pancakes with wooden chopsticks when I was a kid. She made this quite often; her version is gooey inside and crisp outside, with the tomato cooked until almost runny. When I started working, I made this in advance on the weekends to put in my lunch box as it's easy to bring around. In this version I added a few other veggies with mushrooms for variety, and made the batter thicker so it's much easier to flip. You can make these in bulk and store portions of it in the freezer. Usually I eat this as it is because I find it tasty enough, but I've included a dipping sauce to go with it.

NOTES

- My favourite tool for this recipe is a heatproof silicone spatula. It is flexible and won't scratch your non-stick pan.
- The veggies and mushrooms can be replaced with almost anything: kimchi, chilli, leek, bell peppers and more. My favourite combination is kimchi and shiitake.
- Allium-free options: the onion can be replaced with any ingredient you like, though I recommend 2 Tbsp toon paste for a similar taste.
- To make a healthier version, you can replace all-purpose flour with wholewheat flour. You may need to experiment by adding more baking powder and water as wholewheat flour is denser.
- Baking powder can be replaced with baking soda or omitted. Its purpose is to make the pancake fluffier and rounder. If omitted, the pancake will be denser. If you use baking soda, the pancake will be fluffy but will turn out slightly less round.

veggie pancakes

Makes 3 large pancakes

INGREDIENTS
PANCAKE

Oil as needed

$^1/_2$ onion, peeled and finely chopped

0.5-cm knob ginger, peeled and minced

A pinch of salt

3 shiitake mushrooms (or your preferred mushrooms), finely chopped

2 cubes fermented bean curd

$^1/_2$ Tbsp soy sauce

A dash of ground white pepper or black pepper

250 ml (1 cup) water or stock

$^1/_3$ head round cabbage, finely chopped

5-cm length carrot, finely chopped

3 sprigs coriander, finely chopped

$^1/_2$ tsp baking powder

2 cups all-purpose flour

2 tsp white sesame seeds

SAUCE

1 Tbsp oil

6 cloves garlic, peeled and finely chopped (optional)

$^1/_4$ Tbsp + $^1/_4$ Tbsp light soy sauce

60 ml ($^1/_4$ cup) stock

1 tsp dark soy sauce

1 tsp brown sugar

A dash of ground white pepper

Juice from $^1/_2$ calamansi lime or a lemon wedge

METHOD

1. Heat 1 Tbsp oil in a frying pan. Fry onions and ginger with a pinch of salt over medium heat until slightly translucent.

2. Add mushrooms and sauté for a minute until shiitake shrink to almost half their size. Remove from heat and set aside to let the flavours develop.

3. In a medium bowl, mix fermented bean curd, soy sauce, pepper and stock, stirring until the bean curd is dissolved.

4. In a large bowl, combine mushrooms mixture, cabbage leaves, carrots, coriander and baking powder.

5. Add flour and mix until everything is coated with it. While mixing, add the fermented bean curd mixture a quarter at a time, mixing to combine each time. Mix until you don't see any flour. You should get a slightly runny batter.

6. In a non-stick frying pan, heat 1 Tbsp oil over medium-low heat. Pour a third of the batter into the pan. Using a spatula, flatten and spread the batter. Reduce heat to low and cook for 3–5 minutes or until the sides turn slightly brown. Meanwhile sprinkle sesame seeds on the top.

7. To check doneness of one side, push your spatula under the pancake and lift it up slightly. If you can't lift it without it breaking, or if the underside is still pale, it's not done yet.

8. Using 2 spatulas, push them under the sides of the pancake and flip quickly to cook the other side. Add $^1/_2$ Tbsp oil from the sides to ensure the pancake cooks evenly on both sides. Cook for 3–5 minutes and use your spatula to check for doneness. Remove from heat onto a large plate lined with baking paper. Use up the remaining batter to make 2 more pancakes. Let pancakes cool slightly before serving.

9. While waiting for the pancake to cook on each side, make the dipping sauce.

10. Heat oil in a medium pot over medium-low heat and sauté garlic until light brown and fragrant. Add $^1/_4$ Tbsp light soy sauce and let it reduce in the pot.

11. Add stock, the remaining $^1/_4$ Tbsp light soy sauce, dark soy sauce, sugar and pepper. Stir and simmer for 5 minutes to reduce. Add juice, remove from heat, taste and adjust seasoning to what you prefer. Strain to remove garlic, then transfer to a sauce bowl.

12. To serve, cut each pancake equally into 6. Serve warm with the dip. The pancake can be frozen and reheated. The sauce can be kept refrigerated for 5 days.

sweets

hainanese kaya

Makes 300 ml

INGREDIENTS

300 g silken tofu (the type suitable for frying)
100 ml coconut cream
200 ml coconut milk
¹/₄ tsp salt
150 g white sugar
2–4 pandan leaves, knotted
50 g raw or brown sugar (for colour)

METHOD

1. Place tofu in a sieve to remove excess water.

2. Blend the drained tofu in a blender until you get a smooth, creamy liquid. Pour into a stainless steel mixing bowl, then add coconut milk, coconut cream, salt and white sugar. Whisk until combined.

3. Bring a pot of water to a boil over medium heat. Place mixing bowl over the pot and reduce heat to medium-low. Stir continuously for 15 minutes until mixture thickens slightly. Strain into another mixing bowl to remove any lumps. Sit the bowl over the heated pot again and add in pandan leaves.

4. In another small pan, melt raw sugar over medium-low heat, stirring continuously until there are no sugar crystals and a caramel forms.

5. Add caramel to the tofu mixture. Cook for 20–30 minutes, stirring every 5 minutes until mixture is slightly thinner than the desired consistency. The *kaya* will thicken in the refrigerator. Let cool, transfer into a clean container and store in the refrigerator. The *kaya* can be kept for up to 5 days.

NOTES

*   Different brands of coconut milk and tofu will vary in taste. Some tofu yield a jam with a soy aftertaste. Generally, I find that organic tofu gives a stronger soy taste, which I do not prefer in *kaya*. Some brands of coconut milk or cream give a strong coconut aftertaste. Experimentation is needed to achieve the flavour you like.

*   A traditional *kaya* recipe uses white sugar, but you may experiment by replacing it with raw, palm or coconut sugar for a richer caramel flavour and colour. Ultimately, *kaya*, like many Southeast Asian foods, has no recipe set in stone.

*   Salt is important in a sweet recipe, as it not only boosts flavour but also helps to preserve the jam for longer.

*   If an eggy hint is preferred, adding 1 tsp black salt (*kala namak*) at step 5 after removing from heat does the trick.

2

3a

3b

3c

3d

5

Kaya, a Southeast Asian coconut egg jam, is a breakfast staple on many of our dining tables. The smooth, creamy and sweet spread with a milky coconut and pandan aftertaste is universally appealing. Before supermarkets, many households had their own *kaya* formula, often cooked over a charcoal stove for hours. Current vegan versions on the market use pumpkin or sweet potato as base texture — a creative reinvention, but nonetheless it's not quite like the traditional silky smooth *kaya* with rich coconutty notes and the sweet aroma of pandan. The following recipe is a plant-based version of Hainanese *kaya*, which is velvety and has rich caramel notes. Spread on toast with a bit of vegan butter, and pair with local coffee for a traditional Singaporean breakfast.

Kueh dadar is a sweet snack found in Malay, Indonesian and Nonya cuisines. *Kueh* means cake, while *dadar* means omelette or pancake. So, it's a juicy shredded coconut filling wrapped in a piece of pandan-flavoured green crepe. Its unique flavour comes from *gula melaka*, or palm sugar. The green colouring comes from pandan juice or extract; I use only pandan juice here to keep things as natural as possible. One bite of this pancake yields many textures with a subtle sweetness. This plant-based version uses a simple method with common pantry ingredients to replace the egg in the pancake batter, so you will still achieve a tender and fluffy crepe!

kueh dadar

Makes 6 rolls

INGREDIENTS

PANDAN JUICE

5 pandan leaves, chopped

3–4 Tbsp water

FILLING

90 g *gula melaka* (palm sugar chunks), finely chopped

50 ml water

1 tsp salt

1 pandan leaf, knotted

1 tsp cornstarch

30 g ($^1/_2$ cup) grated coconut

CREPE

$^1/_2$ tsp apple cider or rice vinegar

300 ml coconut milk

120 g all-purpose flour

$^1/_2$ tsp baking powder

$^1/_4$ tsp salt

Pandan juice from above or 1 tsp pandan extract

1 tsp oil

METHOD

1. To prepare the pandan juice, blend pandan leaves and water in a blender. Pour blended mixture into a cheesecloth to squeeze out the juice. Set aside.

2. For the crepe, combine vinegar and coconut milk in a mixing bowl. Set aside.

3. Prepare the filling. Place sugar and water in a saucepan. Simmer over low heat, stirring until sugar is dissolved. Add salt, pandan leaves, cornstarch and grated coconut. Cook until mixture is fairly dry and slightly sticky. Set aside to cool.

4. For the crepe, sift flour and baking powder into a mixing bowl, then add salt. In a thin stream, pour in the coconut milk mixture and whisk to combine.

5. Add pandan juice and oil. Whisk until a smooth, runny batter forms. Strain into another bowl to remove lumps.

6. Heat a non-stick pan over low heat. Pour about 60 ml ($^1/_4$ cup) batter into the pan and swirl the pan to distribute the batter evenly. Cook about 15–20 seconds, until crepe is set and cooked. Check by lifting the crepe with a spatula. Remove from heat and let cool. Repeat to use up batter.

7. Place 2 Tbsp coconut filling on a pandan crepe. Roll up and serve. Leftover *kueh dadar* can be kept refrigerated in an airtight container for up to 4 days.

NOTES

- Adding vinegar to coconut milk curdles the milk slightly. It also reacts with baking powder to produces air bubbles, which lift the batter and give the pancake a fluffy and tender texture.

- *Gula melaka* has unique notes of roasted caramel that other types of sugar don't have. However, if you aren't able to get *gula melaka* chunks or blocks, regular coconut sugar works too.

- The filling and crepe should be cooled before wrapping, to prevent moisture from forming inside the pancake and making it soggy.

masala chai muffins

Makes 10–12 muffins

INGREDIENTS
DRY INGREDIENTS

2 cups all-purpose flour

$1/2$ tsp baking powder

1 tsp baking soda

1 cup raw or castor sugar

$1/2$ tsp salt

WET INGREDIENTS

500 ml (2 cups) coconut milk (oat or soy milk works too)

2 Tbsp masala chai spice blend (use more if you prefer a stronger masala taste)

2 Tbsp black tea

$2/3$ cup grapeseed oil or canola oil (or any neutral-tasting oil)

1 tsp vanilla extract or paste

$1/2$ tsp rice vinegar (distilled or apple cider vinegar works too)

METHOD

1. Preheat the oven to 175ºC. In a pot, bring coconut milk, masala chai spice blend and black tea to a light simmer over low heat. Remove from heat, cover and let steep for 20 minutes before straining tea mixture.

2. Whisk tea mixture with the remaining wet ingredients until combined.

3. Mix dry ingredients in a large bowl and make a well in the centre. Add wet mixture and stir gently using a spatula until just combined and no streaks of flour are visible. Do not over mix. I like to gently scrape and lift the batter from the bottom 2–3 times to check for flour streaks.

4. Fill muffin cups equally with batter until three-quarters full. Bake for 15–20 minutes until a toothpick inserted into a muffin's centre comes out clean. Rotate baking tray halfway through baking for even heating.

5. Remove from the oven to a wire rack. Let muffins cool in the baking tray for 5 minutes before transferring onto the wire rack. Serve immediately or keep refrigerated in an airtight container for up to 5 days.

NOTES

- To ensure a good rise and moist texture, make sure your baking soda and baking powder are still active. Test by mixing a pinch of each with vinegar. If they are active, they will bubble.

- Over mixing a batter will burst air bubbles in it and cause gluten to develop, which makes the muffins dense and doughy.

- To prevent the muffins drying out from over-baking, start checking at the 15-minute mark for doneness.

- You can use coffee or any other tea to replace the masala chai and black tea blend here. How about earl grey or cappuccino muffins? Try roiboos for a caffeine-free version.

Masala chai translates literally to "spiced tea". Describing it as the national drink of India is not a stretch. Sold by chai wallahs (tea vendors) on the streets of India, masala chai is an everyday staple for many Indians, and it is now gaining popularity in other countries. I love it for its comforting warmth, which makes it the perfect drink to have during the monsoon season or any cold weather. A friend once gave me a bag of masala chai (spiced black tea) blend from India. I'm no expert when it comes to Indian cuisine, so I used it in something I'm more confident at – baking! I once shared these muffins at a vegan potluck in Singapore and my Indian friends gave their stamp of approval. You can use this recipe to make any flavour of muffins you like!

Pandan is akin to Southeast Asia's vanilla. Singaporeans and Malaysians can easily identify pandan from its sweet and milky fragrance, and characteristic green colour. Traditionally, lots of eggs are used to give this cake its the fluffy and moist texture. In vegan baking, a fluffy cake is a challenge indeed. This recipe was developed after many tries! There's always a limit to how fluffy a cake can be using only plant-based ingredients, but a satisfactory texture can be achieved with the right methods. Here, two methods are used to induce maximum lift in the cake batter – baking soda with an acid and aquafaba.

NOTES

- Let chilled ingredients come to room temperature before you begin. Having different starting temperatures will affect the end product.

- Juice pandan leaves by blending 300 g cut leaves in a blender with 3–4 Tbsp water to get a green paste. Squeeze paste through a cheesecloth bag to extract the juice.

- Cooling the cake upside down contributes to its fluffiness and lightness.Thus the cake should be made using a cake pan with a removable base for easy unmoulding. The cake pans should not have a non-stick coating.

- Replacing any of the ingredients or tools will yield different results.

- It's preferable to use both pandan juice and pandan paste or extract for maximum fragrance and taste. Natural pandan's fragrance is very fickle; it will be reduced after heating yet it offers a depth that only natural pandan can give. You can omit pandan leaves if they aren't available and use only pandan paste or extract, but if it's the other way around, the cake will look yellowish. I personally prefer to use pandan paste over pandan extract as the fragrance is more concentrated. Vanilla paste or essence is also added to give the cake another dimension of sweet fragrance. Without it the cake will taste flatter.

- For this recipe, it's best to make it in an oven you are familiar with. If you really want to nail it, use an oven thermometer as the display's temperature may not be accurate. It's very important to control the temperature during baking, thus keep an eye on the oven after you put the cake in. If the cake is starting to crack, lower the temperature.

pandan cake

Makes two 15-cm cakes or one 20-cm cake

INGREDIENTS

262 g all-purpose flour
1 tsp baking powder
$\frac{1}{2}$ tsp baking soda
1 tsp salt
1 Tbsp vanilla extract
$\frac{1}{4}$ tsp pandan paste
174 ml coconut cream
4 Tbsp pandan juice
174 ml aquafaba
$1\frac{1}{2}$ tsp apple cider vinegar (distilled or rice vinegar works too)
146 g white or raw sugar
3 Tbsp oil

3a

3b

5

METHOD

1. Preheat the oven to 180°C. In a large bowl, sift flour, baking powder and baking soda. Add salt and mix well. Set aside.

2. In a medium bowl, mix vanilla, pandan paste and coconut cream together. Add pandan juice if using. Set aside.

3. In a large bowl add aquafaba and vinegar. Using an electric beater on medium speed, beat mixture until foamy. Increase speed to high and beat until stiff peaks form. It will take about 10 minutes or more for this step.

4. Add sugar gradually and keep beating on high speed until sugar is dissolved and the mixture is thick and glossy. With the mixer running, drizzle in oil and beat until incorporated.

5. Drizzle in coconut cream mixture and beat until combined. The batter should ribbon, meaning any batter that falls from the beater will hold its shape and remain for 4–5 seconds.

6. Add flour mixture a quarter at a time and gently fold in using a spatula. Draw figure eights 5 times with the spatula touching the base of the bowl, then pull it out slightly and mix 5 times with the spatula just touching the surface of the mixture. Stop immediately when you no longer see any flour. Repeat until all the flour mixture is incorporated.

7. Pour batter into two 12-cm cake pans or one 20-cm cake pan, ungreased. Place in the middle rack of the oven and close the door gently. Bake for 25–35 minutes, until a toothpick inserted into the centre comes out clean. After 10 minutes, check on the cake without opening the oven door. If the cake is starting to crack, lower the temperature by 10–20°C.

8. Remove from the oven and let cool upside down on a wire rack for 30 minutes, or until the cake pan is cool enough to handle. Do not touch it while its cooling.

9. Push against the pan's bottom to release the cake onto the wire rack. The cake should be upside down. Remove the pan's bottom by inserting a sharp knife between it and the cake. Let the cake cool completely before slicing to serve. It can be stored in an airtight container for up to 5 days, or frozen for up to a month.

peanut almond cookies

Makes 16–18 cookies

INGREDIENTS

30 g icing sugar

65 g smooth unsalted peanut butter

48 ml neutral-tasting oil (grapeseed, canola, etc.)

130 g all-purpose flour

1/2 tsp baking powder

1 tsp salt

Chinese almond pieces, as needed, for decoration

GLAZE

2 Tbsp non-dairy milk

1 Tbsp syrup (maple syrup, agave, *gula melaka* syrup)

METHOD

1. To make the glaze, mix the ingredients together and set aside.

2. Preheat the oven to 170ºC. Sift sugar into a large mixing bowl. Add peanut butter and oil , then mix until combined and crumbly. The mixture should come together when pressed.

3. Sift flour and baking powder into peanut butter mixture, then add salt. Mix until just combined. Stop when you no longer see any flour.

4. Line a baking tray with baking paper. Shape dough into balls about 15 g each and arrange on the tray. Press an almond into the middle of each cookie and flatten cookie slightly. Brush cookies with glaze.

5. Bake for 12–14 minutes, until cookies are lightly browned. Rotate baking tray halfway through baking for even heating.

6. Let cool completely on a wire rack before serving or storing. The cookies can be kept at room temperature in an airtight container away from sunlight and direct heat for 5 days .

NOTES

- All-purpose flour and icing sugar are crucial in achieving the melting effect. If you wish to make a healthier version of this recipe, you can substitute with wholewheat flour and other types of sugar, but the cookies will lose their smooth melting effect.

- Other types of nut butters work well too, as long as they are smooth and unsalted.

- Do not use strong-tasting oils like olive or coconut oil, which may clash with the main flavours.

- You can use other nuts like cashews, macadamia or regular almonds to decorate. For aesthetic purposes and to maintain a good mouthfeel, it's best to use small pieces, not the whole nut.

These are one of my favourite Chinese New Year cookies to make. They are addictive treats that melt in your mouth gently, releasing their rich, nutty aroma. Because they aren't too sweet, it's easy to eat more than one or two (or maybe the whole bottle, oops!) at a time. Chinese almonds are used to top off each cookie to give a bit of crunch and sweet fragrance. Note that Chinese almonds are different from usual brown almonds. They are smaller and have a sweeter fragrance.

drinks

Masala chai is a traditional Indian spiced milk tea that's sold on almost every roadside in India. One day, I swapped the black tea for coffee in my favourite masala chai recipe just to try it out and was blown away at how magical this blend tasted. Time to spice up your coffee! The warming spices will be sure to power you up in the morning. Of course, you can use this recipe to make regular masala chai by replacing coffee with black tea.

masala coffee

Serves 2

INGREDIENTS

180 ml (³/₄ cup) water

4 Tbsp sugar, or to taste

2 tsp ground coffee

1 tsp grated ginger

³/₄ tsp masala chai blend (spices only)

1 tsp fennel seeds (optional as the masala blend should have some ground fennel)

250 ml (1 cup) soy milk (or oat milk)

125 ml (¹/₂ cup) soy barista milk

METHOD

1. Place water, sugar, coffee and spices in a pot and bring to a boil over medium heat. Simmer and reduce until slightly less than half the original amount of liquid. Slowly add in the milks and stir, bringing heat down to medium-low.

2. Bring to a gentle boil and simmer for 2 minutes. Pour through a fine mesh strainer into a cup. Taste and tweak with more sugar if preferred.

NOTES

- I find that the flavours develop much more after letting the drink sit in a closed tumbler for 15 minutes.

- The difference between normal non-dairy milk and the barista version is that the latter is able to trap more air in the beverage and not separate under heat. This greatly improves the mouthfeel compared to a version using just regular non-dairy milk.

- A high-fat milk brings out the aroma of the spice and caramel richness of the sugar. Thus, please choose the non-dairy milk with the highest fat percentage that you can find. A mix of high-fat soy milk and soy barista creamer gives the best body and richness.

- I've tried this with coconut milk and found that it can overpower the spices.

- Many brands of non-dairy milks can separate under heat, making your chai look like it has bits of white in it. It doesn't look very appetising, but it doesn't affect the taste or texture much. It happens because the milk is brought to a high temperature suddenly. I recommend pouring out the portion of milk needed and bringing it to room temperature using the microwave to reduce the temperature gap. Some brands don't have that issue, so find one that works best for you.

bandung

Serves 2

INGREDIENTS

500 ml (2 cups) water

2 Tbsp dried food-grade rose petals or buds

$1/2$ tsp red food colouring or $1/4$ small beetroot or red dragon fruit, peeled and diced (optional, for colour only)

$1/3$ tsp rose water

3–5 Tbsp sugar, to taste

500 ml (2 cups) soy, oat or almond milk, ideally with at least 3.5 g of fat per 100 ml (use types that are good for adding to coffee and avoid low-fat ones)

Ice cubes as needed

METHOD

1. In a pot, place 250 ml (1 cup) water and dried rose petals or buds. Bring to a boil over medium heat and simmer for 10 minutes or until reduced by half. Remove from heat and add diced beetroot or dragon fruit, or stir food colouring into the mixture. Let cool at room temperature or place in the refrigerator to cool more quickly.

2. Strain the cooled mixture to remove the roses and beetroot or dragon fruit, reserving only the light red water.

3. In a jug, mix the remaining 250 ml (1 cup) water, rose water, sugar, milk and the light red water. Stir until you get a light pink mixture. Taste and adjust with more sugar if you prefer.

4. Fill 2 glasses with ice cubes and pour the *bandung* over. Serve cold and enjoy immediately.

NOTES

- For this *bandung* to taste creamy and smooth, it's important to use thicker and creamier non-dairy milk, thus I've recommended a minimum level of fat for the milk. Generally, non-dairy milks that work well in coffee will do well in other drinks.

- Don't worry about a soy aftertaste, as the rose fragrance is strong enough to cover it. For those who don't prefer soy or almond milk, oat milk is recommended.

- To me, having a source of natural flavour is important for adding another layer of fragrance. If you don't have dried rose petals or buds, you can omit them as the rose water will give sufficient flavour. However, don't overcompensate, as rose water can taste a bit like soap or perfume if too much is added.

- Though the dried rose petals are added to give a natural rose fragrance, they may not be enough for imparting colour. Only certain types of rose can give a sufficient red. Thus adding some colouring (natural or not) will surely give this drink its characteristic pink.

- Rose is known to have health benefits and is used as a remedy in traditional Chinese medicine.

This drink has a special place in my heart. Creamy, rosy, almost neon pink and loaded with sugar, it made me incredibly happy on multiple occasions, especially on hot afternoons, when I was a lower primary school student. For those who never tried this, imagine Turkish Delight in the form of a drink, but less sweet. After going plant-based, I could not find a satisfactory version of the drink, so I decided to make my own from ingredients that are as natural as possible.

mango lassi

Serves 2–3

INGREDIENTS

YOGHURT STARTER (REJUVELAC)

1/2 cup quinoa, rinsed

Filtered or distilled water, as needed

1 large glass jar, enough to hold 1 litre

1 clean cheesecloth with a rubber band

VEGAN YOGHURT

500 ml (2 cups) non-dairy milk

1 tsp sugar (to feed the probiotics)

2 Tbsp rejuvelac

MANGO LASSI

250–300 ml vegan yoghurt

250–375 ml (1 1/2 cups) water, cold or at room temperature

1 ripe mango, peeled and chopped

3

9

METHOD

YOGHURT STARTER

1. Sterilise a jar by pouring boiling water into it and then discarding the water. Use kitchen mitts or towels to handle the jar as it will be very hot. Use this method to sterilise any utensil that will come into contact with the ingredients.

2. Place rinsed quinoa in the jar and fill with 800 ml filtered water. Cover jar mouth with cheesecloth and secure with rubber band. Soak for 10–12 hours or overnight at room temperature.

3. By next morning, the quinoa should have sprouted little tails and the water should have turned cloudy and slightly fizzy. Drain and discard this water.

4. Fill the jar with more water, stir quinoa with sterilised utensils, then drain. Rinse the grains 2–3 times a day using this method until all the quinoa has sprouted. This usually happens within a day at room temperature (25–33ºC), but it may vary.

5. Fill the jar with 800 ml filtered water after the last rinse. Leave for 10–12 hours or overnight. By the next morning, the water will be cloudy and slightly fizzy. Taste some by pouring a little out — do not dip unsterilised utensils into this liquid. It will smell sourish and taste clean, lemony and refreshing with a fermented aftertaste.

6. Strain liquid using a sterilised sieve into a clean airtight jar. This is your rejuvelac. A second batch can be made by filling the jar of sprouted quinoa with filtered water and leaving for 10–12 hours again. Each batch can be kept for up to a week in the fridge.

7. Now you have your starter, let's make the yoghurt. Rinse and drain the leftover quinoa; you can use it as a salad topping!

VEGAN YOGHURT

8. Mix all the ingredients in a sterilised bowl. Cover and leave overnight or for 10–12 hours at room temperature.

9. By next morning your non-dairy milk should have thickened slightly and should smell a bit sourish, just like yoghurt. Now you can make the mango lassi.

MANGO LASSI

10. In a blender, blend everything together. Taste and adjust with more mango, yoghurt or water to what you prefer. If you want a thinner drink, you can add more water. Pour into glasses and serve immediately.

Growing up in a vegetarian family, I loved going to Indian vegetarian restaurants in Singapore. I always had the mango lassi as it was the best thing to soothe a burning tongue! I've yet to find a dairy-free version available, so I've made my own from scratch — that includes fermenting my own dairy-free yoghurt.

If you don't have access to a vegan yoghurt starter, making your own is extremely easy and cheap. All you need is water and quinoa for the starter culture and any non-dairy milk for the yoghurt. The starter is called rejuvelac, a fermented liquid made from water and quinoa. This recipe works best in a warm climate, but if your area isn't as warm as the tropics, don't worry. Simply wrap the jar up in thick blankets.

NOTES

- In fermenting, it's crucial to use clean utensils to prevent other bacteria from breeding. Immersing them in water that has just been boiled (100°C) is a good way to sterilise them. Handle utensils with clean towels or silicone gloves as they are really hot.

- Leftover rejuvelac can be kept for up to a week in the fridge. To maximise the potential of it, you can make more batches of yoghurt. You can portion and freeze yoghurt in an airtight container for up to a month.

- The success of this mango lassi recipe depends highly on the brand of non-dairy milk. Not every plant milk can set to a nice creamy texture. Some may separate, their fermenting time may vary, and their resulting taste will also be different. I've had greatly successful ones with full fat coconut milk and ones that completely separated and failed terribly (almond milk). Blended soaked cashews ferments well too; it gets slightly lumpy but is creamy and thick. Experimenting is highly recommended to find out what works for you!

teh tarik

Serves 2–3

INGREDIENTS

4 tsp tea dust or black tea

300 ml hot water

400 ml barista non-dairy milk, at room temperature

1 Tbsp non-dairy condensed milk (optional, but highly recommended)

3–5 Tbsp sugar, or to taste

METHOD

1. Prepare two large cups with handles, preferably metal with a curved lip for easy pouring. In a pot, steep the tea in hot water, covered, for 10 minutes. Strain into one cup and discard tea leaves. Check the taste — it should be much stronger and more bitter than what you prefer. If not, steep for 5 minutes more.

2. Add barista milk, condensed milk and sugar and stir to combine. With a steady stream, pour the tea back and forth from one cup to the other. Carefully increase the height with each pour in a pulling motion. You want to carefully pull the cups away from each other while the tea is being transferred. The longer the stream, the frothier the tea will become. Be careful not to scald yourself! It took me about 8 pours to get it frothy enough.

3. After getting your desired frothiness, pour into glasses. Serve warm.

NOTES

*   Authentic *teh tarik* is made from tea dust, not whole tea leaves nor fancy Chinese or European tea. Tea dust is ground up tea with vanilla flavouring. It's cheap, lower grade tea made for the masses, and that is the essence of *teh tarik* — an accessible drink for everyone. Some brands offer a *teh tarik* blend, which is the most ideal as it can be brewed strong. Black tea can be a good substitute due to its similar level of strength.

*   Steeping the tea longer than usual is highly recommended to bring out the tea flavour.

*   The choice of non-dairy milk is also important. Barista milk is made to froth up well, while regular ones cannot froth up as much.

*   A bit of non-dairy condensed milk will give the creamy and rich mouthfeel that *teh tarik* has.

In Malay, "teh" means tea and "tarik" means pull. This creamy, frothy milk tea is a popular drink in Singapore and Malaysia, and it's usually found in hawker centres or *mamak* eateries. The milk tea is made by pouring it from one cup to another, often from a great height. This introduces air into the tea, making it lip-smackingly frothy. It's a skill to pour the tea quickly from a height without spilling a drop.

weights and measures

Quantities for this book are given in Metric and American (spoon and cup) measures.
Standard spoon and cup measurements used are: 1 teaspoon = 5 ml, 1 tablespoon = 15 ml,
1 cup = 250 ml. All measures are level unless otherwise stated.

LIQUID AND VOLUME MEASURES

Metric	Imperial	American
5 ml	$^1/_6$ fl oz	1 teaspoon
10 ml	$^1/_3$ fl oz	1 dessertspoon
15 ml	$^1/_2$ fl oz	1 tablespoon
60 ml	2 fl oz	$^1/_4$ cup (4 tablespoons)
85 ml	$2^1/_2$ fl oz	$^1/_3$ cup
90 ml	3 fl oz	$^3/_8$ cup (6 tablespoons)
125 ml	4 fl oz	$^1/_2$ cup
180 ml	6 fl oz	$^3/_4$ cup
250 ml	8 fl oz	1 cup
300 ml	10 fl oz ($^1/_2$ pint)	$1^1/_4$ cups
375 ml	12 fl oz	$1^1/_2$ cups
435 ml	14 fl oz	$1^3/_4$ cups
500 ml	16 fl oz	2 cups
625 ml	20 fl oz (1 pint)	$2^1/_2$ cups
750 ml	24 fl oz ($1^1/_5$ pints)	3 cups
1 litre	32 fl oz ($1^3/_5$ pints)	4 cups
1.25 litres	40 fl oz (2 pints)	5 cups
1.5 litres	48 fl oz ($2^2/_5$ pints)	6 cups
2.5 litres	80 fl oz (4 pints)	10 cups

DRY MEASURES

Metric	Imperial
30 grams	1 ounce
45 grams	$1^1/_2$ ounces
55 grams	2 ounces
70 grams	$2^1/_2$ ounces
85 grams	3 ounces
100 grams	$3^1/_2$ ounces
110 grams	4 ounces
125 grams	$4^1/_2$ ounces
140 grams	5 ounces
280 grams	10 ounces
450 grams	16 ounces (1 pound)
500 grams	1 pound, $1^1/_2$ ounces
700 grams	$1^1/_2$ pounds
800 grams	$1^3/_4$ pounds
1 kilogram	2 pounds, 3 ounces
1.5 kilograms	3 pounds, $4^1/_2$ ounces
2 kilograms	4 pounds, 6 ounces

OVEN TEMPERATURE

	°C	°F	Gas Regulo
Very slow	120	250	1
Slow	150	300	2
Moderately slow	160	325	3
Moderate	180	350	4
Moderately hot	190/200	370/400	5/6
Hot	210/220	410/440	6/7
Very hot	230	450	8
Super hot	250/290	475/550	9/10

LENGTH

Metric	Imperial
0.5 cm	$^1/_4$ inch
1 cm	$^1/_2$ inch
1.5 cm	$^3/_4$ inch
2.5 cm	1 inch

about the author

Joy Yuan is a Singapore-based creative, food and travel blogger. A professionally-trained visual designer and self-taught photographer, she has been creating plant-based recipes for the past decade. She shares her creations online and is often consulted for her knowledge of plant-based food options. She has also appeared on MediaCorp's Channel 8 programme, *Hello Singapore*, to share her recipe for plant-based *bak kwa* (Chinese pork jerky).

Connect with Joy at

http://www.morethanveggies.sg

https://www.facebook.com/morethanveggies/

http://instagram.com/morethanveggies/